THE

LAWS OF DISCURSIVE THOUGHT:

BEING

A TEXT-BOOK OF FORMAL LOGIC.

BY

JAMES McCOSH, LL.D.,

PRESIDENT OF NEW JERSEY COLLEGE, PRINCETON;

FORMERLY PROFESSOR OF LOGIC AND METAPHYSICS, QUEEN'S COLLEGE, BELFAST.

NEW YORK:

ROBERT CARTER & BROTHERS,

530 BROADWAY.

1873.

SMITH & McDOUGAL, Electrotypers, 82 & 84 Beekman Street, New York.

PREFACE.

If we look back half a century we find Formal Logic taught in nearly all the colleges of Great Britain and America, but exercising an influence infinitely less than nothing (to use a phrase of Plato's) on the thought of the countries. Some of the professors and tutors were expounding it in a dry and technical manner, which wearied young men of spirit, and bred a distaste for the study; while others adopted an apologetic tone for occupying even a brief space with so antiquated a department, and threw out hints of a new Logic as about to appear and supersede the old. The lingering life maintained by that old Aristotelian and Scholastic Logic, in spite of the ridicule poured upon it by nearly all the fresh thinkers of Europe for two or three centuries after the revival of letters, is an extraordinary fact in the history of philosophy; I believe it can be accounted for only by supposing that the syllogism is substantially the correct analysis of the process which passes through the mind in reasoning. Certain it is that no proffered logical system has been able to set aside the Aristotelian, whether devised by Ramus, by the school of Descartes, the school of Locke, or the school of Condillac; all have disappeared after creating a brief expectation followed by a final disappointment. It is a remarkable circumstance that the revived taste for logical studies in the last age proceeded from a restoration of the old Logic by two distinguished men, both reformers in their way, but both admirers of the Analytic of Aristotle. I refer to Archbishop Whately and Sir William Hamilton.

Whately first gave his views to the public in an article in the *Encyclopædia Metropolitana*, which was expanded into his *Elements of Logic* in 1826. The publication constitutes an era in the history of the study in Great Britain and America. The admirable defence of the old Logic against the objections of such men as Principal Campbell and Dugald Stewart, and still more, the fresh and apt examples substituted for the dry stock ones which had been in use for a thousand or two thousand years, speedily attracted the favorable attention of the young thinkers of the times; and Aristotle was once more in the ascendant. But while Whately's Elements is an interesting and healthy work, it can scarcely be described as specially a philosophic one. In order to complete the reaction, another thinker had to appear, and subject the whole science to a critical examination fitted to satisfy the deeper philosophic mind of the times. It is a curious circumstance that Hamilton uttered his first oracular declarations on Logic in a severe article on Whately, in the *Edinburgh Review*, published afterwards in his *Discussions*. He embraced the opportunity to bring forth the result of his profound researches, and specially to introduce to the English speaking countries, the Logic which had sprung up in Germany out of

Kant's *Critick of Pure Reason.* Since that date, Logic has had a greater amount of interest collected round it in Great Britain than any other mental science, and has become incorporated with the freshest and brightest thought of the country. The interest in the study has been increased by the *Logic* of Mr. John Stuart Mill, who has evidently felt the influence of Whately in the respect which he pays to Formal Logic, but adheres, as a whole, to the principles of his father, Mr. James Mill, introducing some elements from the cognate Positive Philosophy of M. Comte. Mr. Mill has given an impulse to the study, not by the portion of his work which treats of Formal Logic—which is not of much scientific value—but by his valuable exposition of the Logic of Induction, which would have been of much more value had he left out the constant defences of his empirical metaphysics.

Hamilton is entitled to be regarded as the author of the "New Analytic of Logical Forms"—as he calls it—after the Old Analytic, or syllogistic analysis of the reasoning process unfolded in the *Prior Analytics* of Aristotle. But he has had powerful co-laborers in Dean Mansel, in his valuable edition of Aldrich's *Artis Logicae Rudimenta* and *Prolegomina Logica*, and in Archbishop Thomson, in his *Outline of the Laws of Thought.* The clearest account of the new Logic is to be found, not in Hamilton's own Lectures, which were left in a crude state, but in the *Logic* of Professor Bowen, of Harvard College.*

* It is not my office to criticise the logical treatises of the United States; in fact I have not a complete collection of them. I have observed in some of them, as Atwater's excellent *Manual of Elementary Logic*, a disposition to unite the real improvements of the New Analytic with the established truths of the old Logic.

The New Analytic proceeds directly or indirectly from the metaphysics of Kant. Not that it is to be found developed in the works of Kant, but it is largely grounded on the peculiar principles of the *Critick of Pure Reason;* it rose out of the searching criticism to which Kant had subjected the forms of the Old Logic; and it ramified directly from the logical treatises of such men as Krug and Esser who belonged to the school. It is of a composite structure, resembling the renovations we see in Britain of medieval buildings, the old and the new adapted to each other with wonderful skill, but with an occasional incongruity forcing itself here and there on the notice of the careful observer. I am not convinced that all the parts are likely to be preserved in the shape they now have, or that the Analytic always gives the ultimate expression of the laws of thought; but I am sure it is a valuable accession to the science. Altogether independent of its positive improvements, it has done great service, by the careful examination to which it has subjected the Old Logic—which has come creditably out of the trial. Forms which had become venerable, and, I may add, stiff, from age; and which were inclined to stand on their dignity and acknowledged authority, have been obliged to submit to a sifting scrutiny, which may have shorn them of some of their ridiculous pretensions, but has, at the same time, delivered them from the dry dust which had gathered around them and threatened to bury them. The time has now come for subjecting the New Analytic to a like examination. It has been before us for an age in a half developed form, and for half an age in a fully unfolded shape; and we should now be in a sufficiently impartial position to be able to take from it what is worthy of being retained, and to lay aside what is fallacious or mistaken.*

Had I been satisfied with the peculiarities of the New Analytic, with its fundamental Kantian principles, or its special doctrines, such as that of the universal quantification of the predicates of propositions with its extensive consequences, I would never have published this treatise. On the supposition of the Hamiltonian analysis being correct, I cannot conceive of there being better works written than those of Thomson and Bowen.

The defects and errors of the new Logic are derived mainly from its German paternity. It is infected throughout with the metaphysics of Kant—just as the *Art of Thinking* is with the metaphysics of Descartes, and Mill's Logic with the empiricism of Comte. It ever presupposes, or implies, that there are Forms in the mind which it imposes on objects as it contemplates them ; and it makes the science altogether *a priori*, and to be constructed apart from, and altogether independent of experience. Hamilton quotes (*Logic*, Lect. IV.) Esser with approbation. "It is evident that in so far as a form of thought is necessary, this form must be determined or necessitated by the nature of the thinking subject itself. . . . The first condition of a form of thought is that it is subjectively, not objectively, determined." This fundamental error (so I reckon it) runs through the whole system, and injures and corrupts the valuable truth to be found in the Logic of Hamilton. I acknowledge

* I believe copies may be had of a limited edition of *Philosophic Papers* published by me, and in which I examined Hamilton's Logic. I have reviewed Mill's Logic in my *Examination of Mr. J. S. Mill's Philosophy.*

that there are principles or laws in the mind, original and native; but these do not superinduce or impose forms on objects as we look at them; they simply enable us to perceive what is in the objects. True, there are *a priori* laws in the mind operating prior to experience; but we can discover their nature, and give an accurate expression of them, only by means of careful observation. The science of Logic is to be constructed only by a careful inductive investigation of the operations of the human mind as it is employed in thinking.

In conducting my independent researches in this spirit, I have been thrown back on the old Logic more than even the logicians of the school of Kant have been. But I have been obliged, in order to explain certain operations of thought to which Kant and Hamilton have called attention, to unfold laws which were not noticed by the older logicians.

The main feature of this Logical Treatise is to be found in the more thorough investigation of the nature of the Notion, in regard to which the views of the school of Locke and Whately are very defective, and the views of the school of Kant and Hamilton altogether erroneous. The *Port Royal Logic* complains that the part of Logic which comprehends the rules of reasoning is regarded as the most important; and maintains that the greater part of the errors of men arises from their reasoning *on* wrong principles, rather than from their reasoning wrongly *from* their principles. It is as true of this age as of the seventeenth century, that the attention of logicians has been confined almost entirely to Reasoning. I believe that it is the Notion which requires at this time to be specially examined. I believe that errors spring far more frequently from obscure, inadequate, indistinct, and confused Notions, and from not placing the Notions in their proper relation in Judgment, than from Ratiocination. Even in Reasoning, most mistakes proceed from confusion lurking in the Apprehensions of the mind. We are in more need, at present, of a new analysis of the Notion and the Judgment, than of the Reasoning process. I have found that in the more thorough evolution of the nature of the Notion, especially in the thorough-going separation of the Abstract Notion from the Singular and Universal, we have the means of settling the curious questions which have been started in regard to Judgment and Reasoning in the New Analytic. In this treatise, the Notion (with the Term, and the Relation of Thought to Language) will be found to occupy a larger relative place than in any logical work written since the time of the famous *Art of Thinking*.

I cannot close this preface without referring to the pleasure I had in discussing these questions with successive Honor Classes in Queen's College, Belfast, and expressing my gratification that there have thence sprung—besides others eminent in other departments—three professors occupying important chairs of mental philosophy.

PRINCETON, NEW JERSEY, U. S., *April*, 1870.

TABLE OF CONTENTS.

INTRODUCTION.

PART FIRST.

THE NOTION.

SECTION PAGE

LOGICAL DIVISION.

ANALYSIS AND SYNTHESIS.

LOGICAL DEFINITION.

AIDS TO ABSTRACTION AND GENERALIZATION.

I.—Mental Image, or Phantasm.

II.—Language.

PART SECOND.

JUDGMENT.

CONJUNCTIONS OF PROPOSITIONS, CONDITIONALS, AND DISJUNCTIVES.

IMPLIED JUDGMENTS, OR IMMEDIATE INFERENCES.

PART THIRD.

REASONING.

CONDITIONAL REASONING.

DISJUNCTIVE REASONING.

DILEMMA.

CHAINS OF REASONING, SORITES.

GENERAL REMARKS ON REASONING PROCESS.

SECTION PAGE

FALLACIES.

FUNDAMENTAL LAWS OF DISCURSIVE THOUGHT.

APPENDIX.

INTRODUCTION.

DEFINITION AND DIVISION OF THE SCIENCE.

1. Logic may be defined as the Science of the Laws of Discursive Thought. The matter about which it is employed lies in the mind: it is Thought, which is an exercise of the understanding, the intelligence, or the intellectual or cognitive powers, as distinguished from operations of the motive faculties such as emotion, moral perception or volition. Thought or intelligence may be of two kinds. In some cases we perceive the object or truth at once: as when we see or touch the table before us, as when we know that the shortest distance between two points is a straight line. In other exercises we perceive the thing or truth by a process: from something given we draw something else, as when we argue from certain appearances in the sky that it will be rain, or from the structure of certain strata of the earth's surface that they have been formed in water. This second kind of thought is called Discursive, in which we proceed from something allowed to something else derived from it by thinking; as distinguished from Intuitive Thought, in which we discern the truth immediately. The science which treats of the intuitive operations of the mind is called Metaphysics; the science which considers the discursive acts is Logic.

2. The discursive operations, like all other agencies in nature, proceed in a regular manner, that is, according to laws. By carefully observing the acts of the mind in thinking, we may discover what these laws are, and express them in language or in formulæ. In doing this, we are constructing a science, which is co-ordinated knowledge, as distinguished from the knowledge of individual things as they present themselves. As Logic co-ordinates what it observes, it is a science; it is the science of the laws of discursive thought.

3. There is no definition of Logic in any of the extant writings of Aristotle the founder of the science. Of later logicians some have given a narrower and some a wider definition than that adopted in the text. Some represent it as a pure science; some as a mere art. Some, such as Whately, would have it treat of Reasoning exclusively (omitting the Notion and Judgment), while others would enlarge it so as to make it embrace all intelligence. The definition of the text gives it a rigidly exact field, while it comprises all the mental operations embraced under the laws of discursive thought.

4. It should be noted that Logic does not profess to impart to man the power of thinking any more than Grammar gives him the capacity of speech. Logic finds men engaged in apprehending, judging, and reasoning, and it seeks to unfold the laws involved, just as Grammar presupposes that men can speak, and proceeds to detect the rules of correct speech. And as Grammar by its rules enables persons to express themselves accurately, so Logic by expounding the laws of thought guards against mistakes in thinking. So far as Logic unfolds the laws of a department of our nature it is a science; so far as it supplies rules to guide and guard us in our discursive operations it is an art.

5. As Logic deals with Thought primarily, and looks at Language only secondarily and incidentally, it is thus easily distinguished from Grammar, Rhetoric, and the Science of Language, which all treat of speech, writing or language generally.

6. Discursive Thought may be viewed in its general aspects or in its more special applications. It may be contemplated as directed to objects of any kind, no matter what they be, within or without us; or it may be considered as looking to certain classes of objects: thus it is evident that thinking is somewhat differently employed in mathematical demonstration from what it is when arranging objects in natural history. This gives us the grand division of the science. So far as it treats of discursive operations, whatever be the objects about which it is employed, it is called Universal or more commonly Formal Logic. So far as it considers thinking as directed to special kinds of objects, it has been called Particular Logic or might be called Objective Logic; it embraces such subjects as Demonstration and Induction. This work takes up the former of these.

7. Kant says, "Logic may be considered as two-fold: as Logic of the general (universal) or the particular use of the understanding. The first contains the absolutely necessary laws of thought, without which no use whatever of the understanding is possible, and gives laws therefore to the understanding, without regard to the difference of objects on which it may be employed. The Logic of the particular use of the understanding contains the laws of correct thinking upon a particular class of objects. The former may be called elemental logic; the latter the organon of this or that particular science. The latter is for the most part employed in the schools as a propædeutic to the sciences, although, indeed, according to the course of human reason, it is the last thing we arrive at, when the science has been already matured and needs only the finishing touches towards its correction and completion; for our knowledge of the objects of our attempted science must be tolerably extensive and complete before we can indicate the laws by which a science of these objects can be established. General Logic is again either pure or applied. In the former, we extract all the empirical conditions under which the understanding is exercised, for example the influence of the senses, the laws of the memory, the force of habit, of inclination, consequently also the sources of prejudice, &c." He tells us, General Logic "makes abstraction of all content of cognition, that is of all relation of cognition to its object, and regards only the logical form in the relation of cognitions to each other, that is the form of thought in general." (*Critique of Pure Reason*, Part II., Meiklejohn's Translation.) The distinction between Universal and Particular Logic is

adopted in the text, but with an important modification. Kant makes Universal Logic look at thought apart altogether from content or objects, and supposes that the mind has laws or forms which it imposes on objects. In the text it is supposed that the laws of thought are the laws of the understanding in contemplating objects. Formal or Universal Logic treats of thought, not apart from content, but *whatever be the content, that is, whatever be the objects.*

UNIVERSAL OR FORMAL LOGIC.

8. Let us look at some of the common exercises of Discursive Thought. We have before us a piece of ice. So far as we simply look at it, and perceive its form and color, there is no discursive thought. But we can distinguish between its form and color, or we may think of its qualities, say, its coldness, its brittleness, its transparency; we are now exercising thought upon the object perceived. The mere bodily senses can draw no such distinction. I can not by the eye separate the shape of the piece of ice from its transparency. But on the bare inspection of the object the mind can distinguish between it and any of its properties, or between one property and another. This is ABSTRACTION, a simple and elementary exercise of discursive thought.

9. Again, on looking at two or more objects, we may notice that they resemble each other. An inhabitant of a northern country is travelling for the first time in a southern clime, and beholds a plant such as never fell under his view before, a plant with a leaf like a fan, and on going a little farther he notices another plant of much the same general form. Already he is exercising discursive thought. He was not doing so as long as he was a mere passive recipient of the impression left on the eye by the shape and color; but when he discovers the likeness of the plants he is exercising what is called Comparison. As other like plants fall under his view, he will probably take a farther step ; he will form a class or kind which shall embrace not only the plants which he has seen, but all others, with the points of agreement, which may fall under his notice or that of any other man ; and he will rejoice if some one gives him the name of 'fan palm' to designate them.

The product of these two processes is the Abstract and General Notion. The First Part of Formal Logic considers the Notion, specially the Abstract and General Notion.

10. Suppose now that we have acquired Notions, we may proceed to compare them. By a process like that described above, the traveller may have formed the notion of fig-tree out of specimens of plants of a different order growing in the same region, and he may compare the two kinds of objects of which he has the notion, and he declares the fig to be of a different shape from the palm, and its leaves to be of a different color. When he does so, he is said to be exercising Judgment, which is a discursive operation comparing two or more notions.

The Second Part of Logic treats of Judgment.

11. But Judgment may be of two kinds. In many cases we pronounce a judgment at once on the bare contemplation of two notions. It is thus that, considering the palm tree and the fig-tree, we discern that the leaf veins of the one are parallel, whereas those of the other are curvilinear. But in other cases we cannot discover the agreement or disagreement at once by simply considering the notions we have. Thus we cannot by merely looking at the palm and fig-tree determine how they grow, whether from one seed lobe or two seed lobes · whether from within or by adding rings from without. But we observe that the veins of the palm leaves are parallel, and that those of the fig are reticulated ; and we have learned somehow that parallel-veined plants proceed from one seed lobe or cotyledon (are monocotyledons), and grow from within; whereas net-veined plants spring from two cotyledons (are dicotyledons), and add rings without; and now we are in a position to draw an inference; we argue that the palm, being parallel-veined, is monocotyledonous, and the fig-tree, having netted veins, is dicotyledonous. In drawing these conclusions, we called in a third notion, monocotyledons or dicotyledons, to combine the other two. The process is one of Judgment; but it is to be distinguished from the second operation mentioned above, the Judgment Proper, or what we shall commonly call Judgment. In Judgment we compare two notions directly, and declare their agreement or disagreement; whereas in the process now before us, we compare two notions by means of a third. The process is called Reasoning, Ratiocination or Inference, and its laws are unfolded in the Third Part of Logic.

PART FIRST.

THE NOTION.

1. The operation of the mind in contemplating an object or objects is called Simple Apprehension. The object or objects apprehended constitute the Notion. Sometimes the notion is of an object apart from any relation to others, as 'man' and 'horse,' and is called Simple or Incomplex; sometimes it is of objects in a relation to each other, as 'man on horseback,' and is said to be Complex. In order, however, to its being a Notion, the mind must have brought the objects into a unity of apprehension. 'Man on horseback' is one notion; we contemplate it as one thing.

2. A notion expressed in language is called a Term, as two terms constitute the *termini* or boundaries of a proposition. A term may consist of one word or of several; and one word may contain two terms and express their connection. A word is said to be categorematic when it is capable of being employed by itself as a term, as, for example, nominative nouns, such as horse, dog, deer. Other words, such as adverbs, prepositions, and nouns not in the nominative case, can only form part of a term, and are said to be syncategorematic: thus 'bird on the wing' is one term, though expressed in four words. Again; such words as *sum* (I am existing), *amat* (he is loving), contain two terms, *I* and *existing*, *he* and *loving*, and intimate their relation. In all cases we must look to the thought—to the notion in the mind—and not to the mere words, to determine what is the notion, and what sort of notion it is.

3. All notions are either Concrete, as ice, or Abstract, as coldness. Again, all notions are either Singular, as Aristotle, or Universal, as logician. Combining these cross divisions we get a three-fold division of notions, the Singular, the Abstract, and Universal. It is of great importance in Logic that we know the exact nature of each of these kinds of notion and the distinction between them. Terms are divided as notions are into Singular, Abstract, and Universal, which last are usually called General or Common

THE CONCRETE AND ABSTRACT NOTION.

4. All Notions are either Concrete or Abstract. A Concrete Notion is of objects as they are with an aggregate of qualities. An Abstract Notion is of part of an object as a part, more technically of an attribute of an object. In order to comprehend this distinction we must look at the nature of the original cognitions or apprehensions which we have by the power of intuition which looks immediately on things. In all such we contemplate objects with qualities more or fewer, and the notions thus formed are said to be concrete. The word is derived from *con* together, and *cresco* I grow, and means literally grown together. Some have derived it from *con* and *cerno,* when it means seen together. Either derivation brings out the meaning : in a Concrete Notion the objects with their qualities as it were grow together, and are perceived together. We cannot look on that table without perceiving it at one and the same time as colored and extended : we never can view the color without the colored surface, or the surface without seeing it as having color of some kind. Nor can we by any mechanical or chemical process separate the one from the other. But human intelligence is subtler than any material agent; and we can in thought consider the one without taking the other into account. This process is called Abstraction, from *abs* from, and *traho* to draw, and signifies a drawing off; and an Abstract Notion is of a part or a quality or qualities drawn off from the rest of the object.

5. Abstraction may be taken in a wider or a narrower sense. In the wider sense it is thus defined by Whately: "When we draw off and contemplate separately any part of an object presented to the mind disregarding the rest of it, we are said to abstract that part of it." Thus understood, the part abstracted may exist separately: thus if I speak of the leg of a table in relation to the table, the phrase is abstract; but I may cut off the leg or consider it as it is in itself and without reference to the table, in which case our notion is concrete. But abstraction may be viewed in a more limited way as that operation of mind in which we contemplate an attribute of objects; "by abstract name, I mean the name of an attribute." (Mill.) In this sense the thing abstracted cannot be said to have a separate or independent existence. Thus I can think and reason about the coldness, or transparency, or brittleness of ice, but there cannot be coldness or transparency or brittleness existing separate or apart from the ice or an object that is cold, brittle, and transparent.

6. We may now give examples of each of these kinds of Notions. When I think of a stone, the notion is concrete; but if of heaviness or hardness, the notion is abstract. If I contemplate a fellow-man, the notion is concrete; but if I consider his wisdom, or his learning, or his wealth, the notion is abstract. If I remember a mother, the mental operation is concrete ; but if I muse on her kindness, her care or faithfulness, the process is abstract. If I contemplate God, the notion is concrete—it is God with all his perfections as known to me ; but if I meditate on his infinity, his justice, or benevolence, my idea is abstract.

7. In Abstraction taken in the wider sense, we are much aided by the phantasy or the imaging power of the mind. Having seen an object in its totality I can picture to myself a part, provided that part can be separated. Thus, having seen a plant, I can have an idea of its roots, its stem, its leaves, separately. Having seen a lion, I can picture its head and its jaws distinct from the rest of its body. But these are exercises of the imaging power of the mind, and not of abstraction considered as an act of thought. In forming the Notions of attributes, the picturing power of the mind can be of little service. True, when they are of properties of objects perceived immediately by the senses, it may help us somewhat, thus in thinking of transparency, we may have an idea before us of glass or of ice ; but when the abstractions are high and refined, we can find no image to represent them, and any idea we might fashion, would rather have a misleading influence, at least in rigid thinking. Who can form an idea, in the sense of image, of such abstractions as government, liberty, peace, prosperity, civilization, religion ?

8. It is evident that the mind can draw a number, in some cases an indefinite number, of abstractions from one and the same concrete object. Thus in contemplating a rose, we can abstract its form, its color, its odor, its mode of growth, its stage of growth, its vital functions, its beauty, and I know not how many qualities. From man we may abstract his bodily frame or any part of it, his shape, his size, his reason, his weight, his age, or any of his mental attributes, such as his conscience, his feelings, his sinfulness. It would require hours or days to run over the innumerable attributes we might ascribe to such complex objects as the Hebrew Commonwealth, the Roman Empire, Greek Literature, the English Language, the Political Constitutions of Britain and America. The abstractions made by any one man in the course of a day, or even an hour, are beyond calculation; and we cannot form the dimmest idea of the number fashioned by a man in the course of his life, and still less of those formed by all mankind since they appeared on the earth. Some of these have been embodied in language, but by far the greater number never have been and never will be expressed in words.

9. We cannot have an adequate idea of the process of abstraction, unless we take into account that we may form abstractions from abstractions, and rise to abstractions more and more refined. Perhaps the fittest illustration is to be found in the science of numbers. Number of every kind is an abstract notion: as one, ten, a hundred, or a thousand; you cannot find one apart from one thing, or ten, a hundred, or a thousand apart from ten, a hundred, or a thousand objects. From these notions we may frame higher abstractions as, a, b, c, standing for known quantities, and x, y, z, for unknown. A still higher process of abstraction is involved in the Fluxionary and Differential Calculus and in Quaternions. In thus abstracting it is possible to think of (not to image) an object apart from its qualities. This is the farthest point which can be reached by us; that is, we come to the τὸ ὄν, the Ens or Being of which metaphysicians, beginning with the ancient Eleatics, have made so much, and yet to so little profit, because they have mistaken its nature. When we speak of Being, we do not mean that there is any one existing thing with a separate or independent reality which can be so designated; but simply to point to an attribute which all things have, namely, that they exist.

10. When we come to speak of the General Notion, we shall find that there is an important distinction between the Extension and Comprehension of a Notion. By the Comprehension of a Notion is meant the qualities comprised in it; by Extension, the objects embraced under it. Abstract Notions may be said to have Comprehension, for they embrace qualities; and some have more Comprehension, that is, more qualities, than others. Thus 'intelligence' and 'character,' which include a whole aggregate of properties, is more Comprehensive than 'reasoning,' which is only one form of intelligence, or 'temperance' which is only one element of character. But Abstract Notions can scarcely be said to have Extension, at least as we have above defined it. They are apprehensions, not of objects, but of qualities of objects. At the same time a quality always is in an object, and may be in more or fewer. Thus impenetrability and gravity, which are in all matter, are in more objects than fluidity or redness, which are only in certain forms of matter. The distinction between Extension and Comprehension is one applicable to general, rather than abstract, notions.

From the account now given, the following laws may be derived:

11. *First Law, The Abstract implies the Concrete.*—We have seen that the primary knowledge acquired by us is of objects with qualities more or fewer. By the eye we become acquainted with bodies as at one and the same time extended and colored. By touch, we know things as at once extended and solid. By self-consciousness, we know self as perceiving by the senses, as thinking and feeling. Not only so, but when we recall by the memory, a scene, a person, an event, it comes before us with more than one quality. Even in imagination, the figure or scene comes up in the concrete; we cannot picture to ourselves a body with a shape without also giving it color, or as having color without also conceiving it as extended. Proceeding on these concrete ideas, the mind can distinguish between a whole and its parts, between an object and its qualities, and between one quality and another. It can consider specially any one quality of body, such as its form, its size, its weight, its density. It can distinguish between man as a whole and any one quality of his, such as his bodily strength or stature; and distinguish between any one attribute and another, as between his bodily and intellectual power, between his intellect and his feelings, between any one feeling such as joy, and any other feeling such as sorrow. But we are not to think that because we can thus distinguish between a quality and its object, or between one quality and another, that therefore the quality can exist of itself. The part abstracted implies the whole of which it is a part; in particular the quality or attribute implies an object from which it is taken. The question has often been put, Is there a reality in the abstract notion, and if so, what sort of reality? The answer is that it has a reality in the concrete object or objects, and when it is a quality, as a quality of the object or objects. Hence,

12. *Second Law, When the Concrete is Real the Abstract is also Real.*—In laying down this rule it is of course presupposed that the abstraction has been properly made· that is, that we contemplate a real part of a whole, a real attribute of an object; that when we speak of the whiteness of a lily, the lily is really white. Let, then, the object be a reality, that is, have a real existence, and the quality contemplated has also an existence. True, if the objects be imaginary, say a hundred-handed Briareus in one body, we cannot declare that these hundred hands ever had an existence anywhere except in the imagination of the poet; but if we see a real human being with hands before us, we are sure that the hands exist as well as the possessor of them; and if these hands be strong, that the strength also is a reality. I can separate in thought the beauty of Venus from the person of Venus; but as the person is an ideal creation, so also is the beauty. But, on the other hand, if the beautiful person be a living being, then the form and the color which constitute her loveliness have also an actuality. This proposition is laid down in opposition to those who represent all abstractions as unreal, as imaginary. Some speak of such qualities as existence, beauty, virtue, as mere fictions of the mind, for which it is vain to seek any corresponding reality. It is true all abstractions are creatures of the mind, but when we abstract a real part from a real whole, a real quality from a real object, the abstract has an existence quite as much as the concrete thing.

13. *Third Law, When the Abstract is the property of an object, we are not to regard it as having an Independent Existence.*—Sometimes, indeed, it is a separable part, as the root of a plant; but in this case, when actually separated it is no longer an abstract, but concrete. But when it is a quality such as color, solidity, weight, thinking, desiring, revolving, then it is inseparable from the objects, and has no independent existence—its existence is simply in the objects. Much error has in all ages taken its rise from mistaking abstracts for independent wholes. The Eleatics very properly formed the abstract notion Being, but then they mistook its nature and gave it an existence like the objects, say, earth, or gold, or animals which possess it. All the Greek philosophers erred, less or more, in this respect, giving a separate actuality to the abstractions fashioned by their own acute intellects; and speaking of ideas, substance, physical elements, as if they were agents capable of action like God or individual men. We see a like misapprehension among the scholastic logicians and theologians of the Medieval Ages; and their practical errors came to have a theoretical sanction given them by the sect of the Realists, who gave a confused and mystic reality to the abstract and general notions formed by the mind. The ideal metaphysicians of Germany have in much the same way given to Nothing, Something, Becoming, a place and a power in themselves. Nor have our modern physical inquirers escaped the tendency, for they speak of nature, force, gravity, motion, as if they were entities, acting independently of the objects whose action and mode of action they express.

14. *Corollary.*—It is of great importance to trace up abstractions to the concrete objects from which they are derived. We should thus be saved from the two opposite errors into which we are apt to fall: the error of those who regard abstractions as nonentities, and that of those who give them a distinct being. By following them up to the substances, whether mental or material, from which they are taken, we shall see that they have a reality, and we shall find what is the nature of that reality. Gravitation has no reality distinct from matter, but it has a reality in the stars and planets which it holds in their spheres. Nature is not a separate agency, but is a name for the combined system of things falling under our view in the world. Beauty is a reality, as our esthetic sentiments testify; but has no embodiment except in some beautiful object, though the foolish laudations of some might lead us to think that she has a personality of her own, which she may one day or other reveal to some enraptured boy-poet, or painter, provided he could rise to a sufficiently ecstatic state. Virtue has no separate existence in some ethereal sphere, as we might be tempted to think by the way in which some speak of it; but it has a reality in the voluntary acts of beings possessed of intelligence, conscience and free will. The Alexandrian mystics recommended us to rise to the contemplation of the One and the Good: all very useful and important, we say, provided we seek for it, where alone we can find it, in the One Living and Good God.

15. We cannot close the subject of Abstraction without pointing out the value and the importance of the process. It is involved in all our mental operations which deserve the name of thinking, and in all practical operations which require thinking. We cannot speak intelligently without abstracting, for in speaking about an object we separate it from other things. We cannot perform any practical work without such a process, for in doing it we must distinguish the things falling simultaneously under our notice. It is an essential element in all scientific pursuit; for in science we have to gather the law out of the scattered phenomena of nature, and in order to this there must be the "necessary rejections and exclusions" (Bacon), that is, the omission of the accidental and indifferent. In particular it is by this operation we reach those lofty ideas which philosophy ponders. We draw off from the objects which present themselves to the senses that which is peculiar to the individuals, and we have the idea of matter or material substance. In contemplating bodies we leave out in our thought all other properties except those by which it resists impulse, and we have the notion of solidity or impenetrability. From extended body we omit other ideas, and there remains the idea of pure space. In contemplating ourselves and other intelligent beings, we pass by the peculiarities of the individual, and fixing on the permanent, we have the idea of spiritual substance. We separate the producing power from the events occurring, and we have the idea of potency or causation. We fix on the good or bad qualities of moral agents, and we have the notion of good and evil. These ideas, matter and spirit, substance and quality, space and time, production and power, good and evil, are all reached by abstraction, and like the primary rocks of our earth, they go down the deepest and they mount the highest. Passing beyond those qualities that are fleeting, Abstraction goes on to those that are fixed; brushing aside the contingent, it reaches the necessary; and thus discovers the stationary amidst the flowing, the stable at the basis of the transient, and the eternal underneath the temporary. The mind is thus carried to an elevation where it is above all passing occurrences, which it can survey in the thought that it is above them, while it feels itself planted on a rock which is unmoved amid all mutations.

16. On the other side, let us not in our search after the abstract lose sight of the concrete. Abstract notions do indeed serve most important purposes. They have been wittily called "the ghosts of departed quantities;" they might be more aptly described as the bones, the skeleton, of real bodies. But however essential the skeleton may be to the frame, and however important the study of it may be for the ends of science, it is not in itself an attractive object—except indeed to the anatomist;—one would not just choose to dwell in a chamber full of rattling bones. For scientific and philosophic purposes it is necessary to have abstractions, and these high abstractions; but abstractions cannot promote every good purpose. In particular they are not calculated to call forth feeling or to warm affection into life: it can be shown that emotion is evoked, not by abstract notions and propositions, but by living objects and concrete apprehensions and representations. We do not feel gratitude for abstract kindness, but for the kind deeds of a kind person. Our admiration is excited, not by some grand idea of beauty or sublimity, but by a lovely person or a grand scene. Our love is kindled by the contemplation, not of goodness (as the pantheist would have it) but by a good God or a good man or woman.

17. In order to brace their frame, students should be encouraged to mount the heights of philosophy where they have a wide and glorious prospect opened to them; but lest, by the cold to which they are there exposed, they have the warm current of feeling frozen at the heart, let them ever be ready to return to what they feel after all to be the dearest of spots—the home of the affections. We do not wish to find the youth parting with his youthful feelings; we do not like to see the young man with the face of the old man ; we rather like to see the old man retaining some of his boyish buoyancy. Our noble English tongue has happily been retaining the old Saxon words and idioms which furnish "sweet household words and phrases of the hearth," while it has been adding to them scientific phrases derived from the Greek and Latin languages. On a like principle let students, while seeking to master the deep abstractions, the high generalizations of science and philosophy, cherish their love of the individual, the concrete, the natural: thus only may they be able to keep the simplicity of childhood amid the growing wisdom of age.

SINGULAR AND UNIVERSAL NOTIONS.

18. *All Notions are either Singular or Universal.*—A singular notion is of an object considered as a single object, as Homer, Virgil, Julius Cæsar, Cromwell, Mount Blanc, this horse, that dog, yonder mountain. A Universal is of objects possessing a common attribute or common attributes, the notion being such as to embrace all the objects, real or potential, possessing the common attribute or attributes, as poet, warrior, animal, mountain.

19. Our primary knowledge is of single objects. The boy does not commence with a notion of man or humanity in general, but with an acquaintance with an individual person, say his father or his brother; nor does he start with an idea of womankind, but with a kindly knowledge of his nurse or his mother. It is the same with any other idea he forms, as of sheep, or cow, or dog; he first notices a single animal, and then as he sees others he fashions for himself, or understands as others speak about it, the general notion 'animal.'

20. Abstraction and Generalization, though frequently confounded, are not the same. In Abstraction, we separate in thought a part, an attribute, from the whole. In generalization, we put objects together as possessing the same attributes. In contemplating only one object, we can abstract: thus if it be Alexander the Great, we can consider his military genius apart from his other qualities, such as his impulsiveness. But in generalization we must always have before us a number of objects which we place together by the supposed possession of some common attribute: thus in the notion 'conqueror,' we comprise all the great military geniuses of present, past, and future time. At the same time the two processes are closely connected. Abstraction is always implied in generalization: we can combine the objects in the general notion only by one or more common attributes, which we have therefore abstracted. There may indeed be abstraction, the abstraction of a quality, when there is no generalization, no combining of objects by the quality. But abstraction often leads on to generalization: having observed a number of rocks which bear marks of having been formed in water, we put them in the one class of aqueous rocks.

21. Since the days of Locke, who confounded abstract and general ideas, the distinction between these two kinds of idea has been very much lost sight of. There are metaphysicians, however, who have noticed it. Thus Dugald Stewart: "The words Abstraction and Generalization are commonly, but improperly, used as synonymous; and the same inaccuracy is frequently committed in speaking of abstract or general ideas as if the two expressions were convertible. A person who had never seen but one rose might yet have been able to consider its color apart from its other qualities; and, therefore, (to express myself in conformity to common language) there may be such a thing as an idea which is at once abstract and particular. After having perceived this quality as belonging to a variety of individuals, we may consider it without reference to any of them, and thus form the notion of redness or whiteness in general, which may be called a general abstract idea." (*Elements*, Part I, Chap. IV., § 2, Hamilton's Ed.) Hamilton says: " We can rivet our attention on some particular mode of a thing, as its smell, its color, its figure, its size, etc., and abstract it from the others. This may be called Modal Abstraction. The abstraction we have now been considering is performed on individual objects, and is consequently particular [singular ?]. There is nothing necessarily connected with generalization in abstraction; generalization is indeed dependent on abstraction, which it supposes; but abstraction does not involve generalization. I remark this because you will frequently find the terms abstract and general applied to notions used as convertible." (*Metaphysics, Lect.* XXXV.) But in his Logic he has allotted no separate place to the Abstract Notion, and like all the logicians of the school of Kant, he has no other notion than the Concept or the General Notion. In consequence of this oversight he has not been able to give accurate account of certain peculiarities of thought which he has had the shrewdness to notice. As we advance in this treatise we shall find that we have only to give the abstract notion its proper place, to render a clear and scientific account of certain processes of thought which the old Logic had overlooked, but which the Kantian and Hamiltonian Logic had observed; and that we can thereby remove the hiatus between the Kantian and Aristotelic Logic; and rear out of the two a simple and consistent structure.

22. There is no subject around which there has gathered a greater amount of confusion of thought and logomachy than the General Notion or Universal. It is of vast moment that we should carefully mark the steps involved in its formation.

In order to Generalization two things are pre-supposed. The first is, that objects resemble each other, that is, possess like qualities. In every department of nature there are common properties of form, color, weight, and number which enable us to group objects. The second circumstance is, that the mind has a tendency to seek out and discover resemblances. It is induced to do so by a native tendency, and it is compelled to do so by the circumstances in which it is placed, by the analogies which everywhere fall under our notice, and by being obliged to put the innumerable particulars that would oppress the memory and the understanding into convenient and comprehensible groups. "To shorten its way to knowledge and make each perception more comprehensible, it binds them into bundles." (Locke.) With these preliminaries the operation of generalization is ready to commence.

23. *First Step.*—We observe a resemblance, more or less clearly, among the objects which present themselves. This operation begins in early life. Children soon learn to distinguish, by their points of agreement, human beings from other beings, and the man from the woman, and the child from the adult, and to appreciate practically what constitutes a bird, or a cat, or a sheep, or a goat, or a horse, provided always that they are in the way of coming frequently in contact with such animals. All our lives we are inclined or compelled to discover agreements in the objects or incidents falling under our notice. Sometimes the analogies observed are of a practical kind, and impart to the man who notices them foresight and sagacity; at other times they are of an intellectual or scientific character, and open enlarged views of the connections of things in the universe; while others are more of a literary or poetical nature, and give rise to comparisons, images, similes and metaphors.

24. *Second Step.*—We fix more or less definitely on the points of resemblance. The process formerly noticed is Comparison; that now under consideration is a special exercise of Abstraction. This abstraction is often of a very loose description; that is, we have not accurately defined what the common properties are. We have observed that there is some general resemblance among objects in shape, color, or property, and yet if we were to catechize ourselves, or if others were to question us, we could not tell what it consists in. In other cases, more especially in the classifications of natural science, the points of resemblance are precisely fixed and rigidly defined. A great deal of the confusion of thought and unsatisfactory controversy to be found in the world, originate in men never having definitely determined what are the properties which combine objects in our common notions. Logic promotes clearness of thought by showing that all our concepts are formed by common attributes, and by insisting on our knowing exactly what those attributes are. The common attributes are called technically *Notæ* or Marks by logicians.

25. No absolute rule can be laid down as to which of the steps now referred to is the prior. In most cases there seems to be first a perception of some sort of general likeness, and then the fixing with more or less precision on the point or points of resemblance. But there are cases in which the abstracting process seems to come first. We fix on a quality which is evidently significant, and then put all the objects possessing it into a class. It is thus that in zoology naturalists fix on the possession of a vertebrate column as a characteristic, and in botany the springing from one (or two) seed lobes, and put together the objects possessing the mark fixed on.

26. Whichever of these may come first, both are involved in generalization. But there is more in the process than either or than both of these. These are after all only preparations for the all-important step. Were the operation to stop at this point, there would after all be no general notion. For observe that in the comparison we have only got individuals, more or fewer, and in the abstraction a quality or qualities possessed by individuals. The consummating step has yet to be taken.

27. *Third Step.*—This is the formation of a class or head embracing all objects possessing the common attribute or attributes. In the first step, the comparison, we must have observed or contemplated more or fewer objects possessing points of likeness; still the number was limited. In the second step, the abstraction, we have fixed on some quality or qualities possessed by them in common. But in taking the final step the number of objects becomes indefinite: we must have for convenience sake a head under which we may place not only the objects we have seen, but others we may yet see; in short, all others possessing the quality or aggregate of qualities. It is only when we take this third step that we have a General Notion or a Universal. On seeing only half a dozen buffaloes, we may have been struck with their points of likeness, and may have been able to determine what these were in our minds, specially their shape and mode of motion. But feeling it to be useful, we take the farther step and construct the class 'buffalo,' which must include not only these few, but all others of the same form and habit; not only those now living, but all which have lived and shall ever live; not only so, but all conceivable, all possible buffaloes, the wild oxen of fiction and of the ever active imagination.

28. The Universal is thus, in one sense, indefinite; it includes an indefinite number of objects, we know not how many, all that possess the Marks. In another sense it is definite; it is defined by the Marks. Sometimes, however, the Marks, though supposed to be fixed, are very vaguely apprehended by us: thus the great mass of mankind know what a buffalo is only by some loose idea of its form. We fashion a class called the 'beautiful,' but it has been found extremely difficult to determine what are the common qualities possessed by objects entitled to the epithet, and by no others; and provisionally we can only define it as that which raises certain pleasing emotions within us. Most classes are formed in the first instance without scientific precision, for mere convenience sake. Science as it advances seeks to determine precisely the Marks of classes, and generally to decide what generalizations are worthy of being kept, and what are not, and may therefore be allowed to disappear. This advance in accuracy sometimes breeds confusion from the felt discrepancy between the scientific and popular arrangements. The class heath was probably formed first from the common heather (*Calluna vulgaris*), which now, from the greater precision of the marks, is excluded from it. The correct determination of what constitutes 'fish' has driven out the whale, which is still placed in it in the common apprehension. Such general names as value and money, have a different signification in political economy from what they have in popular language. It is one main advantage of the advancement of thinking and science, that greater precision and fixedness are imparted to the loose, though often useful, generalizations originally fashioned for practical purposes.

As the aim of every science is to discover Laws, and the aim of the science of Logic is to discover the Laws of thought, let us enquire what are the

LAWS OF THOUGHT INVOLVED IN GENERALIZATION.

29. *First Law.*—The Universal implies Singulars. It has been formed out of the singulars. The boy perceives an individual crow before he forms any conception of the class crow, and it is from the sight or contemplation of a number of crows that he forms the general notion. The

Universal notion crow thus throws us back on the individuals entitled to be put under it. It is the same with every other common notion. The Universal is neither less nor more than individuals viewed as possessing certain attributes in common.

30. *Second Law.*—When the Singulars are Real, the Universal is also Real. We perceive a number of bushes before us, and observing that they agree in having the same shape and structure and in having spines, we put them under one head, thorn. What is now affirmed is, that if the individual bushes exist, so also does the tribe. The tribe has a reality in the real bushes, and in the common attributes possessed by them. True, if the singulars are ideal, so may also be the genus. If there be no such beings as ghosts and fairies, then the class cannot be said to have a reality. The question of the reality of the class is thus to be determined by inquiring whether the individuals, and the attributes involved in the classification, have a real existence.

31. *Third Law.*—The Universal has a reality in the Singulars, and in the Common Properties possessed by them, but no Independent Existence. We are not to suppose that the species 'rose' has the same kind of existence as the individual rose : or that 'the beautiful' has the same sort of reality as a lovely star or a lovely woman : or that 'the good' exists as the good God does. The Universal, say rose, beautiful, good, has an existence only in the single roses, and in the objects which are beautiful and good, and in the common qualities combining them. If the Singulars were to cease, the Universal would also cease. Give us individuals possessing a common attribute, and we may form a common notion out of them. Let the individuals have an actual existence, and the notion will have the same, always in the objects and the marks by which they are grouped. In this sense not only what are called natural classes such as Ranunculaceæ, Rosaceæ, Mollusca, but even such generalizations as beautiful, virtuous, clear, high, low, level, united, scattered, have a reality in the common properties of the things joined under these heads. When we say that this rose is beautiful, we mean that it is an object possessing the attributes which bind in one notion the objects entitled to be called beautiful.

EXTENSION AND COMPREHENSION OF GENERAL NOTIONS.

32. According to the account now given, every General Notion embraces two things: it embraces objects, and it embraces attributes. Thus the notion vertebrata comprises objects, viz.: all animals possessing the common property; and it also implies an attribute, the possession by all the animals of a vertebrate column. The former of these is called by logicians the Extension, and the latter the Comprehension or Intension of a notion. The notion Rational Being is said to have Extension, inasmuch as it embraces all objects possessing reason; and Comprehension, inasmuch as all these possess the attribute of reason. The Extension of a Notion is reached specially by generalization as above described; the Comprehension specially by abstraction, that is, by fixing on marks. It is clear that some notions have greater Extension than others: thus man has greater Extension than Frenchman; that is, it embraces a greater number of beings. Some Notions, again, have greater Comprehension than others: thus Frenchman has greater Comprehension than man, for he has all the attributes found in mankind generally, and some peculiar to those who dwell in France. It is evident that the greater the Extension of a term, that is, the number of objects denoted by it, it has the less Comprehension, that is, fewer attributes common to the objects ; and *vice versa*, the more the Comprehension of a term, that is, the number of marks possessed by all the objects, the less its Extension, that is, the fewer are the objects possessing the whole of them.

33. The distinction between the Extension and Comprehension of a Notion, though stated earlier, was introduced formally into Logic in *La Logique ou l'Art de Penser*, by Arnauld and Nicole (1662 A. D.). It is found in a number of logical treatises published in the end of the 17th and beginning of the 18th century. It has been revived by Sir W. Hamilton. It should be remarked that it applies, only with a modification of its meaning, to Abstract Notions (§ 10).

HIGHER AND LOWER GENERALIZATIONS.

34. The objects embraced in a Common Term are commonly combined, not by the possession of one attribute but of several, sometimes an indefinite number. In all such cases we can form higher and higher generalizations. Take the class Dog, it is evident that it includes an aggregate of attributes; so many indeed that we cannot specify them all. Now we may fix on any one of these, and put all the objects possessing it into a group: thus we may fix on the quality of eating flesh, and form the general notion Carnivora. Looking again at Carnivora, we may fix on the possession of a backbone and form the class Vertebrata, and in Vertebrata we may single out the property of organization and form the notion Organized Being. The following table may illustrate the process :

Being.
Substance.
Matter.
Organized Matter.
Animal.

Vertebrata.
Mammal.
Carnivora.
Dog.
Terrier.
Snap.

35. It is desirable to have a nomenclature to express the relation of the classes in this scale, and logicians have supplied us with such. Thus suppose we fix on any class possessing a group or aggregate of properties such as Dog, the logicians would call this Species ; and then the class above it, Carnivora, would be called Genus. But as we may often have occasion to speak of the relation of a greater number of classes we need other phrases, and logicians use Proximum Genus to express the class next above the species, and Subaltern Species the class next below the species. Thus fixing on Dog as the species, Carnivora might be the Proximum Genus, and Mammal the Genus ; while Terrier would be the Subaltern Species. The highest genus which we can form is the Summum Genus ; and the lowest species which we can form, the Infima Species—a point which, however, we can never absolutely fix. If we take all things, the Summum Genus is Being ; if we take merely an order of things, the Summum Genus is the highest in that order ; thus Plant is the Summum Genus in Botany, and Discursive Thought in Logic. It is evident that the Summum Genus can have no species above it, and that the Infima Species has only individuals and no species below it. Looking to the Table we see that the individual has the greatest Comprehension, it has an aggregate of attributes which nobody could specify ; and the least Extension, for it has only one object. On the other hand, the Summum Genus has the greatest Extension, for it includes all objects ; and the least Intension, for it comprises only one attribute. Between these two extremes, the Extension rises as we ascend the scale, while the Comprehension diminishes; and as we descend, the Extension is lessened while the Comprehension is increased. All this follows from the nature of Generalization and the General Notion.

36. These remarks as to relative Extension and Intension presuppose that the same objects are generalized throughout. But mankind form classes among the innumerable objects which present themselves as convenience induces and necessity requires; and it is only in a few sciences that we have such a regular subordination as in the above table. In such general notions as plant, planet, money, revolution, virtue, we have no relation implied except that they may be all placed under some one high genus such as Being. In comparing such notions we can say nothing as to their relative Extension or Comprehension.

37. A notion is said to be Subordinate to another notion when it is included in the Extension of that other: thus 'carnivorous' is Subordinate to 'mammal.' Notions are said to be Co-ordinate when they are species immediately under the same genus: thus mammals, birds, fishes, reptiles, are co-ordinate notions under the genus vertebrate. Notions are said (by Leibnitz) to be Communicant when they overlap each other, as *e. g.* 'poetical writers' and 'writers of tales,' there being some writers of tales who are poetical writers and others who write in prose.

THE SINGULAR CONCRETE, THE ABSTRACT, AND UNIVERSAL NOTION.

38. All notions we have seen are either Concrete or Abstract. All notions we have farther seen are either Singular or Universal. These divisions are made according to different principles or marks. The former is a division in respect of attributes or *notæ,* that is, marks; the mental process involved is abstraction; and it proceeds according to the comprehension of the notions The latter is a division in respect of individuals and classes; the mental process involved is generalization; and it takes place according to the extension of the notions. These are cross divisions; let us combine them. Our first idea might be that we ought to have four kinds of notions. But it so happens, that all notions which are Singular are also Concrete, that is, have an aggregate of attributes; and abstraction is in the Universal as well as the Abstract Notion. We have, in consequence, a threefold division:

1st. The Singular Concrete, as Bucephalus, This Animal.

2d. The Abstract, as Swiftness, Life.

3d. The Universal, as Swift, Animal.

39. The things apprehended in the first may be called Percepts, in the second Abstracts, in the third Concepts. It will be found that all the notions which the mind of man can form, are either Percepts, Abstracts, or Concepts.

40. *The Singular Concrete Notion, or Percept.*—This is the notion with which the mind starts, and from which the two other kinds are derived. It is of objects as they present themselves; and these are known as single, but with a number of qualities. As our observation increases we come to know a greater number of individual objects; and we know each possessing a greater number and variety of qualities, as it were more and more in the concrete. This piece of iron: we may know it first as a mere lump of matter, with a certain shape and color; then we know it as hard; as capable of being melted by heat; as capable of being rusted, that is, combined with oxygen; as capable of being formed into certain useful utensils, and as possessing special magnetic powers. As we thus add one property after another to objects, we are constrained at last to acknowledge that we cannot know all the attributes possessed by any one thing. Who can tell all the qualities possessed by any one metal, plant, or animal?

41. *The Abstract Notion, or the Abstract.*—This is probably the second kind of notion formed by the mind in the order of things. On a concrete object coming before us, we can contemplate a part of it as a part, or an attribute of it: thus having seen Bucephalus we can think of his swiftness. Having an idea of an animal, we can contemplate its life. These Abstract Notions, like all other notions, may be expressed in one word or in several. Thus 'swiftness' and 'life' are abstracts designated by one word. Quite as frequently the notion is embraced in a number of words; and it is of importance that we be able to fix on the one Abstract in the midst of the multiplicity of phrases. When we say, "*to repeat a hundred lines on once hearing them* can be done only by a few," the words in Italics express only one abstract idea. "It is a true saying, and worthy of all acceptation, that Jesus Christ came into the world to save sinners;" here "Jesus Christ coming into the world to save sinners" is one notion, and that abstract. Logic serves a most important purpose when it leads us to detect the Abstract Notion wherever it is found; to perceive exactly what sort of existence it has; ever to go back from the abstract quality to the concrete objects; and to acknowledge in the abstract no other reality than that which is to be found in the objects.

42. *The Universal Notion or Concept.*—To this Notion, or rather thing conceived, I am inclined to restrict the phrase 'Concept' (Begriff in German). The derivation of the word (from *con* and *capio*) requires that it should be applied to those notions, in which we seize on a number of things and bring them into a unity of thought. The Concept thus understood always embraces an indefinite number of objects, all the objects, real or potential, possessing the attribute or attributes which we have fixed on as the ground of the generalization. The Common Term, which is the Concept expressed in language, can be applied to any one of these objects.

43. A distinction of some importance may be drawn between two kinds of Universals—between what I venture to call the Generalized or (simply) General Abstract, and the Generalized or (simply) General Concrete.

44. *The General Abstract.*—In this we have only some one quality, or with qualities involved in it, to constitute the marks of the notion. Thus 'just' is evidently a common term—it embraces all intelligent beings and acts possessing the quality of 'justness.' But it denotes only one attribute, that designated by the term. Of the same description are such classes, as faithful, true, frank, generous, hard, soft, tough, elastic, indeed all adjectives. To such I would apply the scholastic phrase, connotative; they denote an attribute and they connote objects.

45. *The General Concrete.*—In this, a number of the aggregate of qualities to be found in the singular objects, go up into the General Notion. Thus we have in every individual animal a variety of properties which no one can number. Not only so, we have in the general term 'animal' a collection of attributes the whole of which no wise naturalist will venture to specify. Of the same character are man, mineral, vegetable, metal, horse, dog, rose, lily; no one should profess to be able to fix on all the attributes which are found conjoined in every individual of the class. It is not difficult to perceive the difference between these two kinds of notions. Both are Universal, for they include an indefinite number of objects. But in the one the attributes are specified; they are such as faithfulness, generosity, hardness. In the other they are not defined; they consist of an aggregate of qualities found in all the objects.

46. It should be specially observed, that it is classes of this latter description which admit of higher and ever higher generalizations. The boy observes that certain of the animals with which he is familiar resemble each other, and he groups them into such convenient classes as dogs, horses, cows. Then, as he is introduced to the elements of science, he is taught that all these have certain agreements, and that they may be placed in the class quadruped, or mammal. Comparing this with other tribes, such as birds, fishes, reptiles, he finds them all in possession of a back-bone, and he calls them vertebrata. In this way we may mount upward till we come to Being, which denotes existence without quality. Let it be observed that all this proceeds on the circumstance, that as individuals possess an aggregate of qualities, so also may classes of objects. When we come to Being we have risen above the General Concrete to the General Abstract Notion.

47. The circumstance that there are Concrete General Notions has cost logicians a great deal of trouble, and often landed them in inextricable confusion. It was supposed by many of them that a genus or a species was constituted by a certain number of knowable attributes. The schoolmen were ever seeking after a species which would constitute the whole essence of its objects. And this leads me to remark that we believe the schoolmen would not have applied the phrase Species to any class except one with an aggregate of properties. But in natural classes we are not able to point out all the qualities possessed in common by the objects. No man of science will venture to say that he knows all the qualities which go to constitute the essence of metal, or plant, or man.

"Men define a man
The creature who stands frontward to the stars,
The creature who looks inward to himself,
The tool-wright, laughing creature. 'Tis enough;
We'll say the inconsequent creature man,
For that's his specialty. What creature else
Conceives the circle and then walks the square?"

The circumstance that every object, and most classes of objects, possess a number, apparently an infinite number of properties, lands the logician in perplexities and threatens to destroy the symmetry of his system. And were the various properties of things loose and unconnected, it would be impossible to reduce the Concrete Generals to anything like order. As an infinitely worse consequence, it would be found impossible to arrange natural objects into natural classes. For the number of qualities in all objects material and mental being innumerable, we might fix with equal propriety on any one as the ground of the arrangement, and different persons would fix on different qualities, and there could be no agreement among those investigating the kingdoms of nature, or rather we should not be able to speak of the kingdoms of nature. But the God who made all things has, happily for our understandings and our practical convenience, instituted an order among the separate qualities of objects, so that it is possible to arrange them into orders which have such Marks as enable us to fit them into our natural systems. This will be explained in a coming section, when we consider the aids to generalization in the works of nature.

MIXED NOTIONS.

48. We hold that all notions can be referred to one or other of these three heads. At the same time the three may be mixed up with each other in a number of ways. Thus there is the Singular Classified, as 'that statesman,' 'that orator,' 'that general,' 'that philanthropist.' These notions are all singular, but the object is put into a class. Such singular terms are to be distinguished from Singulars Proper, or proper names, such as William Pitt, Edmund Burke, George Washington, William Wilberforce. Again, there is the Singular Collective, or Collective Term, which is in itself Singular, but embraces objects put in a class: thus the 'Forty-second Regiment' is a Singular Notion, but it applies only to soldiers who are classified; 'House of Representatives' cannot be applied to each of the members, but each of the members is a representative of the people. There is also the Singular Abstracted: as when we say Wellington was the conqueror at Waterloo, the term "Conqueror at Waterloo" is Singular, is one thing, but that thing viewed under an abstracted aspect.

49. It is to be specially noticed that very many Terms are used both as Abstracts and Concepts. The tendency always is, when we have seized on an important quality, especially when we have coined a word to express it, to make it the bond of objects, which we join in a class. Thus, having noticed that certain persons possess a quality which we call 'learning,' we form a class called 'learned,' to embrace all who possess the attribute. Quite as frequently we constitute a class by the possession of a number of attributes, known or unknown, and we join all these in one by giving them a name. Thus, without settling what living beings possess in common, we designate what they agree in by the abstract phrase 'life.' It is thus that we have 'generous' to connote the class, and 'generosity' to denote the quality. In these cases the abstracts and concepts are designated by somewhat different though related words. But in many cases the same term may denote both the abstract and general notions. Thus 'virtue' is primarily an abstract term; we have formed it by abstracting a certain quality of intelligent and moral beings. But then the quality has various forms as it appears in different individuals, and at different times, and we classify the diversities and speak of different virtues, such as justice, and temperance, and benevolence, thus making the phrase general. Fine Arts is an abstract term, but it may become a common term with painting, architecture, and sculpture, as subclasses. Pain and pleasure are in themselves Abstracts, but may embrace under them various kinds of sensations, as corporeal and mental enjoyment, and suffering of body, and anguish of spirit. In many cases it is of great importance to determine as to a phrase which may be both abstract and general, in which of the senses it is employed in a given passage or discussion. Such terms as 'substance,' 'quality,' and 'mode,' may be one or other; and in every speculative investigation we should settle in which of the senses we are employing it. Substance is primarily an Abstract, standing for that which abideth in objects material or mental. It stands for a Concept when we speak of two substances, mind and body.

50. Students of logic should notice that there is one class of Abstract Notions which always tend to become general. Verbs are primarily abstracts expressing objects, not in the concrete, but as being, doing, and suffering. But when they are used in propositions they may become general. When we say that "man speaks," the sentence is primarily attributive; it means that man has the power of speaking. But the term 'speaks' may also be interpreted as universal; it may mean that man is in the class of speaking creatures. We shall see, as we advance, that when a verb is used as a middle term in reasoning, it is always to be understood as a universal.

Thus, when we argue that since men speak, and gorillas do not speak, therefore gorillas are not men, we must, in order to the legitimacy of the reasoning, understand 'speak' as denoting all speaking creatures.

51. We form notions of various complexity by accretion and agglomeration. These are called Mixed Modes by Locke. Thus we speak of 'a procession,' implying persons, and a train, and time, and succession. We talk of 'a triumph' implying a battle and a victory, and a display. We join abstracts to abstracts ; we speak and write of 'the triumph of excellence,' of 'the defeat of wickedness,' of 'the reward of righteousness' and 'the punishment of evil,' of 'the beauty of natural scenery,' of 'the hopefulness of spring,' of 'the gloominess of winter,' of 'the madness of passion,' 'the terrors of despair.' We join general with abstract notions. Thus we have the abstract idea 'wickedness,' and we have the general notions 'human,' and 'demoniac,' and we talk of 'human wickedness' and 'demoniac wickedness.' We have expeperienced 'joy' and 'sorrow,' and we know what 'elevation' is and what 'depression' is, and we speak of 'the elevation of joy' and 'the depression of sorrow.'

52. But whatever be the genesis of our notions, in the end they come to be either Percepts, or Abstracts, or Concepts. To avoid confusion of thought and misapplication of terms, it is of moment that we should be able to say as to every given notion, under which of these heads we are to place it. When we say "Shakespeare's Plays are the best in the English language," the one notion "Shakespeare's Plays" is Singular Concrete (Collective), and the other "the best in the English language," an Abstract. When we say "Logic is the science of the Laws of Discursive Thought," the two terms "Logic" and "the science of the Laws of Discursive Thought," are both Abstracts. When we say "the hearts of sufferers can be won only by love," the two notions "hearts of sufferers" and "can be won only by love" are both Universal.

PRIVATIVE NOTIONS.

53. We have seen that in Universals, objects are bound into one by the possession of Marks. But we may also unite objects by the absence of Marks. Thus we say that all quadrupeds are vertebrates; and we say of mollusca, that they are invertebrate. The former of these notions is called Positive, and the latter Privative. Logicians have remarked that a Positive and Privative Term divide among them the universe of being, that is, all objects must either be vertebrate or invertebrate. But when interpreted properly, this means simply that each object must either possess or not possess a given attribute. It does not imply that the non-possession of that attribute is a proper mark by which to join objects. There would be no propriety in putting all objects which do not possess a back-bone, say thought, the soul, probity, dress, planet, into the class invertebrata—which should be applied only to those portions of the genus animal which we wish to distinguish from vertebrates. It should be remarked that some seemingly privative phrases really imply a positive Mark: thus the phrase 'immortal' implies not merely that the object does not die, but that it lives forever; and the term 'infinite' may be held as meaning more than merely the absence of bounds, it involves the occupation of all space and all time.

CONTRARY AND CONTRADICTORY NOTIONS.

54. Positive and Privative Terms are said to be Contradictory; that is, they are such that we cannot conceive them as applied to the same object at the same time, such as existent and non-existent, organic and inorganic. Contrary Terms, called by some Incompatible, are such as might be conceivably applied to the same object, but cannot, in fact, be so applied, such as good and bad, light and darkness, cold and hot.

RELATIVE NOTIONS.

55. These are derived, not from a quality in one object, but from the relation of one thing to another. When we speak of the objects under this relation, they are said to be Correlative. Thus we have sovereign and subject, parents and children, husband and wife, master and servant. The one of these implies the other. They are connected by the ground of the relation (*fundamentum relationis*). The phrases themselves are Universals (General Abstracts); the relation, say that of sovereignty and subjection, is abstract; for *relatio non est per se reale, sed per suum fundamentum.*

LOGICAL DIVISION.

56. In generification, that is, in the formation of common notions, we rise from singulars to classes, and from lower classes to higher. But after the classes have been fashioned by ourselves or others, we may reverse the process and descend from higher classes to lower

This operation is called Logical Division, which may be defined as the process by which we spread out a genus into its co-ordinate species. It is to be distinguished from Partition, which consists in separating an individual object into its parts ; as when we sunder a plant into stems, roots, and branches. Logical Division takes up a common notion, such as plant, and spreads it out into acotyledons, monocotyledons, and dicotyledons. To every such sub-class the name of the higher class may be applied ; thus we speak of plants, monocotyledonous, and dicotyledonous, and in the same science of Geum urbanum and Geum rivale. It is evident that Division proceeds specially according to the Extension of a notion ; and it involves Comprehension only so far as Extension implies Comprehension. The rules are :

57. *First Rule.*—We must proceed according to a Mark or Marks added, and according to the same Mark or Marks throughout. We have seen that in the ascending process of generification, we leave out marks ; thus in ascending from dog to carnivora, we leave out every property of the dog except that of eating flesh. In the descending process of division we add marks. Thus in dividing plants, we add the property of growth by seed-lobes, and put those growing from one seed-lobe under one head, and those growing from two, under another. Discursive Thought is divided into the Notion, Judgment, and Reasoning, according as we exercise thought in apprehending, in comparing the things apprehended directly, or comparing them by means of a middle term. As in our divisions we proceed on a principle, so that principle should always be clearly understood and very commonly be enunciated. What should be the Marks fixed on must be determined by the nature of the objects, and the scientific or practical end we have in view at the time. Here Logic can be of little use to us ; but then it serves an important purpose by insisting that there must be Marks. It does more : it requires that we proceed throughout on the same Marks. In dividing mankind, we may proceed on various principles : as on the principle of race, into Caucasian, Malay, Mongols, Negro ; on the principle of enlightenment, into savages, uncivilized and civilized ; of religion, into Christians, Mahometans, Pagans. But it would be wrong to flit from one of these to another, and divide mankind into Christians, Mahometans, and savages ; or into Europeans, Americans, Pagans and Mahometans. The logician would err were he to divide discursive thought into the term, the proposition, and argument ; for in the first he would be proceeding on the principle of language ; in the second, on that of thought. Arrangements violating this rule are called 'cross-divisions.' "It is a useful practical rule, whenever you find a discussion of any kind very perplexing and seemingly confused, to examine whether some cross-division has not crept in." (Whately).

58. *Second Rule.*—The species must make up the genus, or, as it is otherwise expressed, the dividing members (*membra dividentia*) must make up the whole. This rule would be violated were we to divide vertebrate animals into quadrupeds, birds, fishes, and reptiles ; for there are animals—man, for instance—included in vertebrata, but not in the division. We shall see, in treating of Judgments, that Immediate Inferences can be drawn on the principle of division ; but this can be done only on the assurance that the division is complete. There is often a fallacy lurking in imperfect divisions. Thus the Eleatics argued that there could not be such a thing as motion, for that the motion must either be in the place where it is, or in a place where it is not, neither of which is possible ; whereas there is a third supposition that it may have been from the place where it was, to the place where it now is. Another sophism proceeds on the same mistake. It is argued that academical honors are useless, inasmuch as they are not needed by those who have a taste for study, and that they have no effect on the idle, and such as are indifferent to mental improvement. Here it is tacitly assumed that all students must belong either to the diligent class or the idle class; whereas there may be a large intermediate class, not altogether hopelessly idle on the one hand, nor with confirmed habits of application on the other, and these may be influenced by academical distinctions.

59. *Third Rule.*—The dividing members must exclude one another. This rule would be violated were we to divide lines into straight, curved, circular, and elliptical, or notions into singular, concrete, abstract, and universal—for abstract notions are also singular. He who neglects to attend to the rule, will offend every person of correct judgment, and confuse the minds of those who do not see the fault of the division. The preacher violated it when he proposed proving a particular doctrine from reason, and from revelation, and the testimony of Paul; his division should have been from reason and from revelation, and under the latter, he might have said, especially from the testimony of St. Paul. The barrister transgressed it when he talked of establishing his point by moral law, by the law of the land, by Act of Parliament, and precedent; for Acts of Parliament and precedents are included under the law of the land. The Chinese are said to furnish a ludicrous example of this error in their division of the race into first Chinese, then men, and then women. The error arises commonly from introducing subordinate species and not adhering to co-ordinate species. It will often happen that a division contravening any one of these rules will also violate all the others. Thus a librarian who would arrange his volumes as books of prose, poetry, morals and religion, as proceeding on no principle, would never be able to make up the whole, and would find his divisions running into inextricable confusion.

60. *Fourth Rule.*—There should be a due subordination of classes—*Divisio non faciat saltum.* The contents of elaborate treatises are commonly distributed into Books, Chapters, and Sections. We should never be able to arrange the vegetable kingdom if we proceeded to distribute plants as they cast up into roses, oaks, lilies, lichens; nor the animal kingdom if we began to divide them into horses, dogs, leopards and lions. Naturalists fix on a regularly ascending or descending series of divisions and sub-divisions; thus Agassiz arranges the animal kingdom into Branches or Types, Classes, Orders, Families, Genera, Species.

61. These rules are of value in the sciences, especially those which are concerned with classification, such as Botany and Zoology. True, they do not tell us how we are to arrange the organic world, for this must be done by a careful observation and induction of the facts; but they lay down certain stringent laws of thought which must be attended to in the classifications formed. They may also be of great service in the construction of essays, papers, sermons, and discourses of every kind. It is not necessary in all cases to announce the division. Some people have argued that such an announcement must make the composition stiff and formal, and is apt to damp the curiosity of the reader or hearer who ought to be kept awake by a desire to know what is coming. On the other hand, it is argued that when our end is not merely to please or tickle the fancy, but to impart instruction, it is of importance to announce the divisions and subdivisions, which will be found greatly to aid the memory and comprehension. The question of whether we should or should not lay down a formal division is tc be decided by the end we have in view, whether it is simply to amuse or interest for the time, or to convey important truth which we expect to be recalled and pondered.

ANALYSIS AND SYNTHESIS.

62. Analysis (from ἀναλύω, I unloose), is that process in which we separate in thought, a concrete object or a complex abstract notion into its parts or qualities. Analysis is always performed by means of Abstraction, but the two differ. In Abstraction we mentally separate any quality; in Analysis we spread out the qualities which make up the whole. It is seldom we can unfold all the properties of a concrete object, and not always that we can fix on all those of a complicated notion. There are times, however, when we can bring out to view the attributes involved in an abstract which we have fashioned. Thus we analyze discursive thought into thought as directed to objects whatever they be, and thought as directed to special classes of objects; and the former we analyze into Simple Apprehension, Judgment, and Reasoning. We thus see that Analysis is not the same as Division. In Division we take a class and distribute it into sub-classes; in Analysis we take a concrete object, or more frequently a comprehensive abstract, and spread out its qualities. It may happen that where an abstract term is also a common term, division and analysis coincide. Thus, as 'Discursive Thought,' and as 'Notions,' 'Judgments,' and 'Reasoning,' are at one and the same time Abstracts and Concepts, it is of little moment whether we call the distribution of them a division or an analysis—whether we say that we divide or that we analyze the notion into percepts, abstracts, and concepts.

63. Having found the parts by Analysis, we may join the parts to show that they make up the whole by a process which is called Synthesis (from *συντίθημι*, I place together). When we can prove that the parts by their junction constitute the whole, the synthesis is a confirmaation of the accuracy of the previous analysis. It is clear that in the study of a new or hitherto unexplored subject, we must begin with analysis. But after we have made a successful analysis, we may then advantageously employ synthesis in corroborating the previous analysis, and the synthetic method in expounding the science which treats of the objects. Thus in chemistry, having shown what the elements of bodies are, we may then take up these elements one by one, and show how we can explain by them the composition of all bodies. Thus in Logic, having ascertained by analysis that thinking consists in Simple Apprehension, Judgment, and Reasoning, we then consider each of these, and show how they together constitute the discursive operations of the mind. Whately has imparted a great interest to his *Elements of Logic* by introducing us to the subject by an analysis of the reasoning process, and then proceeding to develop the science in the synthetic method.

64. Analysis and Synthesis used to occupy a much more important place in Logical treatises than they now do. They were represented as the main instruments in the investigation of nature. It was, in fact, very much by mental analysis and synthesis that the philosophers of ancient Greece and Rome and the medieval logicians and theologians proceeded in their physical speculations. The instrument is now seen to be Induction, and Deduction joined with it in certain walks of inquiry. But it can be shown that analysis is an important element in Induction. Phenomena falling under the senses or our observing faculties are always concrete or complex, and we must so far separate the things which are joined together before we can reduce them to a law, or even observe them. Hence Bacon says, we must begin Induction by the "necessary rejections or exclusions;" and Whewell says by "the Decomposition of Facts."

It can be shown also that Synthesis may act an important part in Deduction. But these questions carry us into Inductive Logic.

LOGICAL DEFINITION.

65. By definition (ὁρισμος) is meant in the most general sense "a description which manifests the nature of the thing defined." Logical Definition is to be distinguished from mere verbal explanation: as when a child does not understand what is meant by perspicuous, and you say it means clear; or when you say that salubrious means tending to produce health. It is the province of a dictionary to give the explanation of words. But in definition we must manifest the nature of the thing defined.

66. We can logically define only those notions in which there has been a process of discursive thought; that is, abstract or general notions. We cannot, properly speaking, define a singular notion, for we cannot manifest its nature by bringing to view all its attributes, the attributes being innumerable. All we can do is to give some marks of the individual, technically called a description, sufficient to detect the object and distinguish it from others. We have such a description in the "Hue and Cry" sent after a criminal, "five feet eight, light hair, blue eyes, a scar on the right cheek." We have such descriptions, sufficient to enable us to recognize them, of towns, rivers and mountains, in our traveller's guide-books.

67. It has been remarked by many philosophers that there are some notions which cannot be defined. It will be found that these are abstracts: they are qualities which cannot be resolved into anything simpler, such as sweetness, sourness, pleasure, pain. We can give no idea of them to one who does not know already what they are;

all that we can do in explaining our meaning is to appeal to our experience of them. But while we cannot define them so as to manifest the nature of the thing, we can make a great many affirmations and denials regarding them. Thus we can say that such a sour taste is produced by vinegar; that a purple color proceeds from the union of yellow and blue rays. Much information can often be given by specifying the objects in which the quality is to be found: thus we can say that pleasure and pain are affections of beings endowed with sensation. We can always make an indefinite number of negative statements regarding these simple ideas, to face misap prehensions or misrepresentations, as that pleasure does not consist in the mere possession of wealth, or the means of sensual gratification. But there are cases in which we can give a definition of an Abstract Notion; being complex we can analyze it into its constituents. Thus we can define Discursive Thought as an exercise of mind in which we proceed from something given or granted, to something else founded on it.

68. It is disputed among metaphysicians whether such ideas as those of Extension, Power, Moral Good, are to be put under the same head as those of pleasure and pain; that is, under the head of original ideas, revealed to us by the senses or primitive perceptions. When asked to define virtue, or moral good, we can only say virtue is virtue, good is good. But then we can make an indefinite number of negative propositions regarding them: thus we say that virtue or good does not consist in mere happiness; and that the relation of cause and effect does not consist in invariable antecedence and consequence.

69. We should always be able to define a General Notion. We have seen that objects are brought together into a common notion by means of the possession of a common attribute. Now we can bring out this attribute in definition, and in doing so, we indicate the bounds of the common notion, and thus what it is as distinguished from other things. It is evident that definition proceeds specially according to the Comprehension of a notion.

70. *First Rule.*—We must bring out a distinguishing attribute of the notion defined. When this is done there is always a true definition. When this is not done there is no proper definition. When we say man is a rational being, we have given a sufficient definition; for rationality is a characteristic quality not found in inanimate nature, or in the brute creatures. When we say Logic is the science of the discursive laws of thought, we have brought out a distinctive mark, distinguishing the science from all sciences with which it might be confounded, such as Ethics and Metaphysics. As to what is a distinguishing property of a notion, this must be determined not by Logic, but the sciences which deal with the objects. But Logic insists on our fixing on such a property. Herein is the person trained to logical habits distinguished from others. How often do we find the uneducated man struggling to give expression to what he knows in a loose way, and failing. You ask him what Logic is, and he answers a branch taught in our colleges; what Arithmetic, and he says a branch taught in our schools; what Language, and he says a means of expression—as if there were not other branches taught in colleges and schools, and as if there were not other ways of expressing thought. The person disciplined in Logic knows that in giving a definition he must fix on a distinguishing attribute, and he seeks for it and is not satisfied till he finds it.

71. And here it is of importance to remark how it is that what we have called the General Concrete Notion is defined. It is evident that we may not be able to bring out all the attributes common to the notion, for we may not know what they are. It is enough in such cases to specify one characteristic which may be a sign of the others. We may not be able to mention all the attributes found in mammals; but it is a good definition when we say that "they are animals suckling their young," for this brings out to view a quality common to the whole class, and a quality which is the sign of others.

72. *Second Rule.*—The definition must be adequate to the notion, neither wider nor narrower. If we defined grammar the art of speaking a language with propriety, the definition would be too narrow, for grammar treats of writing a language as well as speaking. If we defined it as the science of language, it would be too wide, for grammar does not discuss all the scientific questions connected with language. If we defined Logic as the science of our intellectual nature, it would be too wide; if as the science of reasoning, it would be too narrow.

73. N.B.—The best test of this property of a good definition is, that the subject can take the place of the predicate, and the predicate of the subject, without any change. Thus defining a straight line as the shortest distance between two points, we can say the shortest distance between two points is a straight line. We can say truly 'all poets are men of genius,' but this is no definition, for we cannot say all men of genius are poets.

74. *Third Rule.*—It is expedient to give the genus as well as a characteristic quality. When we do this we are said to define by *genus* and *differentia*—that is, characteristic quality. This cannot always be done, as there may be notions which it is difficult to put into a genus in any way fitted to clear up their nature. But when it is possible we should give both the *genus* and the *differentia*, as by the one we show wherein the notion agrees with others to which it is most clearly allied, and by the other we show wherein it differs from the notions with which it might be confounded. In giving a genus it is expedient to give the *proximum genus.* Thus we may define Ethics as "the mental science unfolding the laws of man's moral nature;"

in which "mental science" is the *proximum genus*, putting ethics under the same head as psychology, logic, and metaphysics; and "unfolding the laws of man's moral nature" is the *differentia*, separating it from these departments of knowledge.

75. Some important practical rules may be laid down as to the language in which the definition should be given. The general rule is, that the definition should always be clearer than the thing defined. More particularly (a) the definition must not be expressed in ambiguous or figurative language, as Aristotle's definition of Motion, "the act of being in potency, so far as being in potency."

(b) It must not contain covertly the name of the thing defined, as when we say abstraction is a process in which we abstract or draw off, or that life is the sum of the vital functions. (c) When the class has positive attributes, the definition should not be put in a negative form. Those who say that infinite is a positive quality, should give a better definition of it than when it is said, it is that which has no bounds. Naturalists no longer give invertebrata as the name of a scientific class to be placed alongside of vertebrata.

AIDS TO ABSTRACTION AND GENERALIZATION.

76. In the employment of abstract and general notions, the mind must always have some sign before it. This sign may be

I.—A MENTAL IMAGE OR PHANTASM.

77. We have occasion, let us suppose, to speak of the rose tribe of plants; as we do so, we may notice that we have a loose idea, in the sense of image, of a plant which may have as many as possible of the characteristics of the rose without those of other plants, such as the tulip or the lily. Or we have occasion to think of plant generally, and we fashion a figure, very possibly with axis, branches, and leaves (though there are plants without these), which may stand for all plants. The image may also aid us in our abstractions. When we think of great size, we picture a huge bulk ; when of tallness, we picture great length ; when of transparency, ice or glass with light shining through ; when of wealth, a heap of money ; when of dignity, a man of imposing form and address ; when of pomp, a dazzling show ; when of martyrdom, a person suffering for the truth ; when of mirth, a man laughing ; when of sorrow, a person crying. It is by help of such images, that children, savages, rustics, in fact the great body of ordinary men and women, are able to form abstracts and concepts. When such phantasms can be formed, they always render our thinking more lively, and therefore more interesting and better fitted to call forth emotion. Our pictorial, who are always our most popular writers, help our understandings by furnishing concrete pictures of abstract notions, and thus enable us to carry on our thinking more easily and pleasantly—often, it has to be added, more obscurely and confusedly.

78. These ideas or phantasms are not to be understood as constituting the abstract or general notion. It is usually said of our common notions that they are inadequate. But this is not true of our concepts as exercises of thought ; they may be regarded as adequate, for they are of things joined by common attributes, the concept embracing all objects possessing the common attributes. But it holds good of the ideas considered as mental pictures : we can form no correct image of gravity, or hardness, or weight, or indeed of any quality. Nor can we fashion a full phantasm of a concept, for the objects are joined by a quality or qualities abstracted, and the objects are innumerable. We cannot form a correct picture of man in the general, for if we make him white we do not include the Negro or Red Indian; if we make him black we leave out the Caucasian race; and if we make him neither black, nor white, nor red, we leave out the whole of these three tribes of mankind. In all cases the phantasm is to be regarded as a mere sign or representation of the result of elaborative thought. It is not of the mere phantasm that we make affirmations or denials, but of the things for which it stands as apprehended by the mind. In certain cases the mental image when used as a sign, is quite sufficient to enable us to think accurately, that is, when it stands for ideas not far removed from the singular and the concrete. But when the notion becomes more and more abstract or general, more especially when it is the idea of spiritual objects or qualities, or when it is a composite one, the formation of a mental picture becomes more and more difficult, and at last is seen to be altogether impossible. Who can form an image, for instance, of law, of truth, of right, of government, of learning, of civilization? When we have occasion to think of such things, we must call to our aid external Signs, and especially Language.

79. Locke confused himself on this subject by not distinguishing between the image and the notion, both of which were embraced in his favorite phrase 'idea,' which, however, he commonly used in its literal sense as image. In forming our idea of man or humanity, persons leave out that which is peculiar to the individuals, they leave out of the complex they had of Peter and James, Mary and Jane, "that which is peculiar to each, and retain only what is common to them all." (*Essay*, Book III, iii, 7.). Bishop Berkeley saw the absurdity of this view, and not seeing the way out of it, landed himself in nominalism, which thence descended to Hume, Stewart, and Whately. "The mind having observed that Peter, James, and John resemble each other in certain common agreements of shape and other qualities, leaves out of the complex or compounded idea of Peter, James, and any other particular man that which is peculiar to each, retaining only what is common to all, and so makes an abstract, wherein all the particulars equally partake, abstracting from and cutting off all those circumstances and differences which might determine it to any particular existence. And after this manner, it is said, we come by the abstract idea of man, or, if you will, of humanity or human nature; wherein, it is true, there is included color, because there is no man but has some color; but then it can be neither white nor black, nor any other particular color wherein all men partake. So likewise there is included stature; but then it is neither tall stature nor low stature, but something abstracted from all these." Such considerations show that we cannot form an idea of man in general in the sense of a mental picture. But they do not prove that we cannot form an intellectual conception of objects joined by common properties, the conception including all the objects possessing the properties. We are thus thrown back on the distinction drawn by Aristotle between the phantasm (*φαντάσμα*) and notion (*νοήμα*). The difference between them and yet their relation are accurately expressed by him when he says that the notion is not the same with the phantasm, and yet is never without the phantasm. *Νοήματα τινὶ διοίσει τοῦ μὴ φαντάσματα εἶναι, ἢ οὐδε ταῦτα φαντάσματα, ἀλλ' οὐκ ἄνευ φαντάσματων.* (*De Anim*, iii, 7.)

II.—LANGUAGE.

80. Language may be defined as the expression of our mental actions and affections by means of words spoken or written. The primary benefit derived from it arises from its being a means of communicating with our fellow-men, and thus enabling us to convey to them our varied thoughts and feelings, wants and wishes, and to have theirs imparted to us. This is the first and final end of language, subordinating every other, and determining in a great measure the changes which it has undergone throughout its whole history. But this is not the aspect under which we are required to contemplate it in this work, where we view it simply as the instrument of discursive thought.

81. *First.*—Language is advantageous, inasmuch as it is a sign and register of the abstractions and generalizations which mankind are ever forming. We have seen that all men are led by a native intéllectual tendency, and by the circumstances in which they are placed, to separate and to combine the objects they meet with; to distinguish between a thing and its qualities; to observe the relations of things, and then put the things which are related into a class. Many of the distinctions thus drawn, and groupings fashioned, are valuable only for the moment; but others are of permanent importance, and should be carefully preserved; and this can be done only by a name, by what is technically called Denomination. A simple illustration or two will enable us to understand this. A merchant, say a druggist, has in his warerooms a large number of miscellaneous articles lying promiscuously on the floor; as long as they are in this state he feels that he has not absolute command of them; and so he fixes on some ground of distribution and arranges them in shelves or drawers on which he puts some kind of mark or label. Having done so, he and his assistants find that they can at once lay their hands on the article they require. Or, a naturalist enters a country the flora of which has hitherto been unexplored. As he views the profusion before him his first act is to observe, and his second is to classify; but unless he take a third step, he is made to feel that all his researches are likely to be valueless, if not to himself, at least to others; he has to give a name to the plants which he has put into a class. This name finds its way into botanical books, and becomes the index of the genus or species to students of every country and of all coming ages. These illustrations show us the benefit of names in the business of life and in natural science. But they serve a like, and, in most cases, a vastly more important purpose in regard to all the multiplied operations of the mind; preserving them, when they might otherwise be lost, for our own use and that of others; it may be handing them down to all posterity, or spreading them over all civilized nations. In contemplating the objects which present themselves in the world without, and the still more wondrous world within under its divers moods and impulses, mankind fashion an infinite variety of thoughts, which can be preserved and profitably employed only by the instrumentality of language.

82. *Second.*—Language puts us in possession of the abstractions and generalizations which have been made by other men. In saying so we do not refer to the circumstance that it is not so much by personal observation as by intercourse with others, that it is by the instruction imparted by teachers, companions, and our fellow-men generally, and by books ancient and modern, that we acquire by far the larger portion of the knowledge possessed by us; for this proceeds from the primary use of language as a means of communication. A reference is made under this head, not to the information thus conveyed, but to results of discursive thought embodied in words and phrases. It should be observed indeed, that the abstractions and generalizations must first have been formed before they could be expressed in language. But the name being given it becomes at once and forever a sign of the idea. On the word being brought under the attention of the young, they ask what is meant by it, and are thus put in possession of the thought which it may have cost so much pains to elaborate. An intelligent youth hears the phrases 'conservation of physical force' and 'correlation of physical forces' employed, and on inquiring into their signification, he is taught that the amount of force, potential and actual, in the universe, is always one and the same, and cannot be diminished or increased by any human means, and that all the physical agencies, mechanical, chemical, electric, and vital, are modifications of that one force. Or he hears the word 'æsthetics' used, and is thus introduced to a science which seeks to investigate the laws, subjective and objective, of the beautiful and sublime. What is thus seen so clearly in science is also manifested in moral and practical matters. Some one saw very keenly that there is a vast amount of pretension in the world, and that there are persons who recommend as great and good what is not really so, and gave expression to his perception in the word 'humbug;' and the phrase goes down to posterity because of its felt truthfulness. Some terms spring up by a sort of accident and are retained because found to be useful; there is, for example, the word 'cabal,' made up of the names of persons who were supposed to have formed a party combination, and the phrase has kept its place ever since, because an ever recurring feature of human nature. The British soldiers who had been in the wars of Gustavus Adolphus, brought back with them certain terms such as 'plunder,' 'life-guard,' and 'furlough,' which have ever since been retained in our tongue. Thomas Carlyle, with that vigorous grasp of intellect and atrabilious temperament by which he is distinguished, in order to show his contempt for those who are ever fawning on the great, gave expression to what he observed and felt in the word 'flunkeyism,' a phrase likely to go down to all future generations. To an American custom we owe the phrase 'stump-orator,' so descriptive of a style of speaking which cannot otherwise be so briefly characterized.

83. The occupations, the tastes, the habits, indeed the whole character of a people, are apt to embody themselves in their language. It is said that in Arabic there are 500 names for a lion, 200 for a serpent, 80 for honey, 400 for sorrow, and 1000 for a sword; and it seems certain that there are 5744 relating to the camel. The French have given us the words 'finesse,' 'prestige,' 'ennui,' 'foible,' 'chagrin,' and many others descriptive of their character and experience; and the English have given them in return 'jockey,' 'club,' 'sport,' and the phrase 'comfortable,' so expressive of genuine English feeling. The Scotch have designated one feature of their national character by the word 'canny;' and the Irish have expressed one of their national traits by the phrase 'blarney.' A number of words which have of late come in upon us with such weight and gravity, such as standpoint, God-consciousness, claim Germany as their fatherland.

84. In holding intercourse with each other, persons fashion or modify phrases in accordance with the native tendency of thought, and in order to promote mutual convenience. This remark holds good, not only of individual words, but of the structure of language generally. Hence we have in so many tongues prefixes, suffixes, and reduplications; the gender, number, and case of nouns, and the moods and tenses of verbs. These modifications, say declensions and conjugations, invented or adopted in the first instance for convenience sake, become in the next generation the means of introducing the young to the distinctions of sex, and quantity, and time; to the more important relations of things one to another; and the contingency, the certainty, and necessity of events. Language thus becomes an important means of training the youthful mind to an acquaintance with the habitual and useful modes of human thought and contemplation.

85. It is not possible to express the higher forms of thought in the language of a people low in the scale of intelligence. In the Iroquois there is no word for goodness in the abstract, they have only a word for good man. In the Mohican there is no verb for 'I love,' the forms involve the subject as well as the action, 'I love him,' 'I love you.' In those islands which the London Missionary Society has done so much to elevate, there was one word for the tail of a dog, another for the tail of a bird, and a third for the tail of a sheep, but no word for tail in general. In Chinese there are terms for elder and younger brother, but none for brother. Christian missionaries found great difficulty in fixing on an unexceptionable word in that tongue for God, and disputed among themselves as to which of the available phrases was the least objectionable. The fixed forms of that language and its want of inflections have, I doubt not, acted with other causes in keeping that people in a stationary condition for thousands of years. Notwithstanding the strong attachment of the people to the Gaelic, the Welsh, and the Irish, it is desirable that these tongues should give way as speedily as possible in favor of the English, with its advanced intelligence, its refined sentiment, and noble literature. The circumstance that one tongue, and this enriched by the thoughts of the highest science, philosophy, and theology, is used in all the schools of the United States, has helped more than any other agency to produce a unity of belief, character, and aims, which keeps the people together in spite of the many disturbing causes which might make them fly asunder.

86. The line of thought we are pursuing is fitted to show the advantage of being acquainted with more than one tongue. Every educated people has fashioned thoughts for itself and embodied them in peculiar phrases ; hence the difficulty of translating the words of one tongue into precisely synonymous phrases in another. By learning the language of a race, we come into possession of their mode of thought, which is to us fresh and original. Ennius used to say that he had three hearts (the heart being reckoned the seat of intelligence) because he knew three languages, the Greek, Latin, and Oscan. The Emperor Charles V. declared that a person is as many times a man as he knows a number of languages. Often do we find in other tongues a phrase embodying an idea which never occurred to us; or we are delighted to fall in with the expression of an idea which had floated in our minds without our being able to give it an exact shape. It sometimes happens that an inaccuracy or confusion of thought in one tongue may not occur in another tongue, to which we have only to look to have our ideas cleared up. Thus the distinction between the phantasm and the general notion, drawn by Aristotle and known in the middle ages, was lost sight of by the English-speaking nations for ages after the time of Locke, who confounded them and expressed them both by his favorite phrase 'idea.' Of late years the distinction has been revived in our country greatly to the benefit of philosophy and specially of logic, by scholars who noticed, in perusing works of German speculative philosophy, that the two had been distinguished.

87. Modern European thought has been greatly benefited by the study of the ancient classical languages, which commenced in the fifteenth century and has been continued to the present time in all the higher seats of learning. We have thereby got good not merely from the faultless models of brevity, elegance, and taste presented by the Greek and Roman writers, but from the very words themselves and the ideas embodied in them. We have derived a like—in some respects a higher—advantage from the introduction of Eastern thought, especially from the Divine thought received from the Scriptures with their elevated views of God and holiness—we get the very idea of holiness, or separation from sin, from the Word of God, there being no such idea in the writings of Greek or Roman authors. The English language has been farther enriched by ideas conveyed by the Italian from the time of Spencer to that of Milton; by the French in the last century, and by the German in this. Our language, like our race, is a happy mixture of very diverse elements: while we have as the basis the phrases and inflections of the old Saxon tongue, we have made free additions from the Greek and from the Latin (either directly or through the Norman French) which have introduced us to a more advanced style of thought, and a more refined mode of life.

88. *Third.*—Language constrains us to give a form to thought which would otherwise be loose and vague.

" Language is a perpetual Orphic song,
Which rules with Daedal harmony a throng
Of thoughts and forms, which else senseless and shapeless were."

Let us try to understand how this takes place. We enter a large factory; we see the complicated machinery, the work done, and the persons doing it, and we are filled with a general astonishment. Our ideas meanwhile may be very indeterminate. But we meet with one acquainted with the work, and he names the parts one after another, the machinery, and the raw materials, and the products at the various stages of advancement; we now feel that our notions are becoming clearer. Or, we know that after we leave the work we shall be obliged to describe it to a friend, and we try to get names for the varied apparatus, and to reduce what we have seen to heads. Now there is a like process going on, often without our noticing it, in the formation of our higher and subtler thought. In being obliged to express our thoughts, we have to make them definite in order to bring them within the forms of settled language. This is specially the case when we have to write out our thoughts. "Conference," says Bacon, "maketh a ready man," that is, ready to express intelligently the thoughts that occur; "and writing an exact man," that is, having leisure to put his thoughts into shape, and knowing that others will have time to examine them, he has to make them assume a more accurate form. How often does a student imagine that he has an idea of a subject about which he is reading, or on which he has heard his teacher lecture, till such time as he is examined on it, or has to write definitely upon it, when he discovers how vague his notions have been. It is the great advantage of systematic examinations and of essay-writing, that they force the student to understand his topic in order to his being able to unfold it in language spoken or written. The interrogative or maieutic method of Socrates was specially fitted to accomplish this end, by constraining the person questioned to give his thoughts a definite shape and order.

89. The determinate moulds supplied by language, into which to pour our solvent thoughts, are of various kinds. Sometimes they are abstractions or analyses, which enable and constrain us to decompose concrete or complex objects. More frequently they are common notions, under which we are led or obliged to put single objects or lower classes.

90. It is commonly said that language is first synthetic, and then analytic. The more correct statement is, that it is first concrete, that is, stands for things with an aggregate of qualities, and then becomes more and more abstract, that is, designates common qualities, or objects joined by common qualities. First a word is fixed on to denote an object; then it is modified by additions, by affixes or suffixes, or otherwise, to denote related objects; and then it becomes a root or norm of other phrases clustering round it with allied meanings. It is in its growth that language becomes synthetic in the proper sense of the term, that is, words are joined to express a complexity.

91. As thought and language make progress, more and more is taken in from the void (τὸ ἄπειρον, as the old Greek philosophers called it); the waste becomes measured and fenced in; and those who come after must accommodate themselves to what their predecessors have settled. It thus comes that while language aids thought, it tends at the same time to limit and restrain it. In using the tongue provided for us, we must fall in with the forms which it furnishes. The analyses and generalizations of words have, as it were, laid down rails on which our thoughts run easily and rapidly, and we are induced to travel on these accustomed ways instead of striking out new paths for ourselves. This may be one reason why the earliest poets of a country—such as Homer and Æschylus in Greece, Lucretius in Rome, and Dante in Italy, and Chaucer and Shakespeare in England—are often the freshest; they looked at things with their own eyes, and not as other men through the eyes of others. This may be one of the ends served in Providence by the confounding of old tongues and the necessary formation of new ones; as when the northern nations came in upon the Roman empire, and Norman French became mixed with the Saxon; the same purpose is served as by the mixture of races—the hereditary sameness is disturbed and we have a new progeny with fresh life and new characteristics. Still, the incidental evils arising from a language being settled, are as nothing compared with the advantages proceeding from a cultivated tongue, which provides innumerable analogies and analyses to stimulate and guide thought. Any evils which might arise from a slavish adherence to fixed inflections and routine phrases, are to be overcome by our forming the resolute determination to make language our useful servant without allowing it to become our arbitrary master.

92. *Fourth.*—Language lightens thought by being used as a symbol. When we think of objects not present, we must always have some representation of them before the mind. This, we have seen, may primarily be a mental image; thus when we are thinking about mothers generally, we fix on some one mother, say our own, and leave out as many of her peculiarities as may make the idea stand for mothers generally. But we have shown that this phantasm must always be inadequate to represent an attribute, or a class comprising an indefinite number of objects ; and as the generalizations become wider and the abstractions more refined, and when different abstractions are mixed with each other, it may be impossible to form a picture resembling the reality in the remotest degree. Besides, even though we could fashion an adequate image, it would be sure to distract the mind by calling it away to adventitious circumstances. These inconveniences can be obviated only by the use of external signs, and particularly of language.

93. Let us notice how external symbols are fitted to lessen the labor of thinking. They do so inasmuch as they render it unnecessary to take notice of the unnumbered objects which go to constitute a class; as they save us from conceiving the attributes which combine the objects in the class ; and from thinking of the peculiarities of the individuals. To illustrate by an example. In the natural arrangement of plants there is a subclass, *thalamifloræ*, from *thalamus* and *flos* (flower) ; its characteristics are said to be " calyx and corolla present, petals distinct, inserted into the thalamus or receptacle, stamens hypogynous." Now had this tribe of plants not received a name, we should have been obliged, every time we thought or spoke about them, to represent to ourselves or enumerate to others their various characteristics, and we should have been forced to endeavor to conceive of the numberless plants belonging to the class ; and as we tried all this, we should have found ourselves distracted and overwhelmed. This burdensome work is avoided by using the phrase *thalamifloræ* to stand for the whole tribe.

94. As feeling the convenience of it, and as being endowed with the organs of speech, and the mental capacity and inclination to employ them, man naturally and spontaneously betakes himself to words, to stand for thoughts and things. "It is not necessary, even in the strictest reasonings, that significant names which stand for ideas, should every time they are used create in the understanding the ideas they are made to stand for. In reading and discoursing, names are for the most part used as letters are in algebra, in which, though a particular quantity be marked by each letter, yet to proceed right it is not requisite that in every step each letter should suggest to your thoughts that particular quantity it was appointed to stand for." (Berkeley.) In many processes of thought, the attention seems to be very much fixed on the verbal sign ; and conception comes to be what Leibnitz calls Symbolical. Words come to be used like algebraic symbols, a, b, c, which stand for quantities without our thinking of any particular quantity, like counters which represent money, like bank-notes which stand for gold. The mind yields willingly to this state of things, as feeling how much the memory and the power of imaging and apprehending are thereby eased. We do not choose every time we use such words as liberty, independence, order, civilization, virtue, commonwealth, church, religion, to think of all that is comprised in them. We pass them on as the banker gives away a hundred pound note, or a hundred dollar bill, without thinking of the gold it stands for ; or as we receive it without conceiving how many articles of utility or of comfort it would purchase. Language is thus a species of stenography by which the mind lightens its labors and makes its higher efforts less irksome.

95. *Fifth.*—It follows as a corollary, that by means of language we can carry on thinking to a greater extent than we should otherwise be able to do.

We do not allow indeed, that language, or even that external signs, are necessary to thought. It is forever rung in our ears by certain writers, that there could be no reasoning, no thought of any kind, without language. Dugald Stewart goes so far as to maintain, that "without the use of signs our knowledge must have been confined to individuals, and that we should have been perfectly incapable both of classification and general reasoning ;" and "lays it down as a proposition which holds without any exception, that in every case in which we extend our speculations beyond individuals, language is not only a useful auxiliary, but is the sole instrument by which they are carried on." This is a very extreme position, proceeding on a doctrine which tends to degrade the human faculties, and which has been most eagerly maintained by those who derive all men's ideas from sensation. In opposition to it I lay down the counterpart statement, that without thought language could not be fashioned, could not be understood, could not be intelligently employed. "Parrots," says Locke, "will be taught to make articulate sounds enough, which yet are by no means capable of language. Besides articulate sounds, therefore, it was farther necessary that man should be able to use these sounds as signs of internal conceptions, and to make them stand as marks of the ideas within his mind." "From whence it follows," says his critic, M. Cousin, "that language is not the product of sounds, that is to say, of the organs and the senses, but of the intelligence ; 2. That the intelligence is not the product of language, but, on the contrary, language is the product of intelligence ; 3. That the greater part of the words having, as Locke well remarks, an arbitrary signification; not only are languages the product of the intelligence, but they are even in great part the product of the will ; while in the system that has prevailed both in the school of Locke and in a school altogether opposed to his, intelligence is made to come from language ; in the latter, without much inquiring whence language comes, in the former, by making it come from the sensation and the sound, without suspecting that there is a gulf between the sound considered as a sound and the sound considered as a sign, and that what makes it a sign is the power to comprehend it, that is, the mind, the intelligence."

96. Two circumstances show that the mind can reason without language. One is, that we can point out cases in which there is reasoning without words. An experienced seaman looking on the sky, which to our eye seems so calm, utters something about a storm. We ask what he means, and his explanation only renders the subject more confused. But we know what he intended when a few hours after we see an angry sea, and find the waves lashing on the vessel as if bent on sinking it. There has certainly been a process of reasoning, and the logician could state it in syllogistic form ; but it is doubtful whether language has been of any use in enabling him to conduct it. Another circumstance is, that infants reason. Referring to the view of those who deny the possibility of reasoning of any kind without the aid of general terms, Dr. Brown says : "As if the infant, long before he can be supposed to have acquired any knowledge of terms, did not form his little reasonings on the subjects on which it is important for him to reason, as accurately probably as afterwards, but at least, with all the accuracy which is necessary for preserving his existence and gratifying his few feeble desires. He has, indeed, even then, gone through processes which are admitted to involve the finest reasoning by those very philosophers who deny him to be capable of reasoning at all. He has already calculated distances, long before he knew the use of a single word expressive of distance, and accommodated his induction to those general laws of matter of which he knows nothing but the simple facts, and his expectation that what has afforded him either pain or pleasure, will continue to afford him pain or pleasure. What language does the infant require to prevent him from putting his finger twice in the flame of that candle which has burned him once? or to persuade him to stretch his hand, in exact conformity with the laws of optics, to that very point at which some bright trinket is glittering on his delighted eye? To suppose that we cannot reason without language, seems to me, indeed, almost to involve the same inconsistency as to say that man is incapable of moving his limbs till he have previously walked a mile." (*Lect.*: XLVII.)

97. Such considerations show that,

> "Thought leapt out to wed with thought,
> Ere thought could wed itself to speech."

And then have we not all had thoughts and sentiments which, so far from being the product of words, we have felt it to be impossible to translate into words, and we have reason to complain,

> "Oh dearth
> Of human words, roughness of mortal speech."

Our men of profoundest thought and deepest feeling, have ever striven to rise above human phrases and gaze directly upon realities.

> "Words are but under agents in their souls;
> When they are grasping with their greatest strength
> They do not breathe among them."

This does not prove, on the opposite side, that even such thoughts might not be made more definite, and therefore more thoroughly significant, by being expressed in words; it simply shows that language, with all its refinements, does not come up to the extent and variety of thought.

98. It should be freely allowed that very much of our thinking is carried on by means of language. We have already had before us the circumstances which furnish an explanation. Though, in the order of the formation of language, the notion comes before the name, yet it is commonly by the name, at least in countries richly supplied with common terms, that the notions are first gained. The name and the notion are thus indissolubly associated in our minds, so that there is never the one without the other. Then, as feeling the notion to be complex and a burden upon our conceptive power, we prefer thinking by the simple word rather than be at the trouble of apprehending all that is involved in its signification.

99. While we can think and reason without words, we are all the better of language in every case, and in many complicated operations we should be lost as in a labyrinth without signs of some description. Even in the apprehending of abstract and general notions, we are the better of names; but we especially need them when we come to compare our notions, either immediately in Logical Judgment, or mediately in Reasoning. The botanist, let us suppose, is comparing two classes of plants, one whose characteristics have already been given, and the other thus described :—"Sepals 4, deciduous, the two lateral ones gibbous at the base; stamens 6, tetradynamous." How troublesome would it be to specify these marks every time we had occasion to consider or speak of the relation of these two tribes of plants. We are saved from all this by having a name for each of the groups; the one is called *thalamifloræ*, and the other *cruciferæ*, and the relation between them is expressed by saying that the *cruciferæ* are an order under the sub-class *thalamifloræ*.

100. And if language be useful in judgments in which we have only two notions, it is still more advantageous in reasoning, in which we have three notions. In order to see the utility of symbols in reasoning, we have only to consider that all inference, except in a few simple cases, implies one or more class notions. It proceeds, as we shall see, on the principle that whatever is predicated of a class, may be predicated of all the members of the class. In all cases there is a class notion in the argument, and in many cases all the three notions compared, minor, major, and middle, are general. How cumbersome should we find it, were we obliged in every argument, to consider the indefinite individuals and the common marks that combine them in every concept. And when in our ratiocinations there is not only one argument but a chain of arguments, each containing one, two, or it may be three concepts, with their innumerable individuals and their combining attributes, I believe the mind would feel itself utterly bewildered and oppressed without the use of symbols to stand for the classes.

101. In thinking with the assistance of words, we can pass as far beyond thought conducted by mere mental signs, as by numbers we go beyond counting with the fingers, and by algebra beyond arithmetical computations. The transmission of messages by the electric telegraph hundreds of miles in a few seconds, is an outward picture of the rapidity with which the most remote and recondite thoughts may be brought into communion by the refined phrases of a cultivated language. "Though we should be capable of reasoning without language of any sort, and of reasoning sufficiently to protect ourselves from obvious and familiar causes of injury, our reasonings in such circumstances must be very limited, and as little comparable to the reasoning of him who enjoys all the new distinctions of a refined language, as the creeping of a diminutive insect to the soaring of an eagle. Both animals, indeed, are capable of advancing, but the one passes from cloud to cloud, almost with the rapidity of the lightning which is afterwards to flash from them, and the other takes half a day to move over the few shrunk fibres of a withered leaf." (Brown.)

102. *Sixth.*—It is one of the special advantages of language that it helps thought to make progress. This is very happily brought out by Sir W. Hamilton: "A sign is necessary to give stability to our intellectual progress—to establish each step in our advance as a new starting-point for our advance to another beyond. A country may be overrun by an armed host, but it is only conquered by the establishment of fortresses. Words are the fortresses of thought. They enable us to realize our dominion over what we have already overrun in thought—to make every intellectual conquest the basis of operations for others still beyond. Or another illustration: You have all heard of the process of tunnelling, of tunnelling through a sand-bank. In this operation it is impossible to succeed unless every foot, nay, almost every inch, in our progress be secured by an arch of masonry, before we attempt the excavation of another. Now, language is to the mind, precisely what the arch is to the tunnel. The power of thinking and the power of excavation are not dependent on the word in the one case, nor on the mason-work in the other; but without these subsidiaries neither process could be carried on beyond its rudimentary commencement. Though, therefore, we allow that every movement forward in language must be determined by an antecedent movement forward in thought; still, unless thought be accompanied at each point of its evolution by a corresponding evolution of language, its further development is arrested. Thus it is that the higher exertions of the higher faculty of Understanding, the classification of the objects presented and represented by the subsidiary powers in the formation of a hierarchy of notions; the connection of these notions into judgments; the inference of one judgment from another; and, in general, all our consciousness of the relations of the universal to the particular, consequently all science strictly so denominated, and every inductive knowledge of the past and future from the laws of nature: not only these, but all ascent from the sphere of sense to the sphere of moral and religious intelligence, are, as experience proves, if not altogether impossible without a language, at least possible to a very low degree."

INCIDENTAL DISADVANTAGES OF LANGUAGE.

103. Bacon directed the attention of modern thinkers to that subject in illustrating the Idola Fori, or those which arise from the intercourse of mankind one with another. "Though we think we govern our words, yet certain it is that words, as a Tartar's bow, do shoot back upon the understanding and do mightily entangle and pervert the judgment." The subject thus opened has been prosecuted by Hobbes, by Locke, by the French school of Condillac, by Stewart, by Whately, and others, some of whom trace almost all errors to the influence of language. Locke has dilated on this subject (*Essay*, B. III.), and has offered many valuable cautions, but often exaggerates the evils. "He that shall well consider the errors and obscurity, the mistakes and confusion that are spread in the world by the ill use of words, will find some reason to doubt whether language, as it has been employed, has contributed more to the improvement or hindrance of knowledge among mankind." When men's ideas are confused, the language they employ will also be confused, and thus increase the confusion—just as when a master does not thoroughly organize his household, the servants instead of aiding him will throw everything into disorder. Examples of the evil influence of terms, are often taken from imperfectly formed sciences, material or mental; but there the error has sprung from the state of the department of knowledge; and when the science is properly constructed by its appropriate means, inductive or deductive, it soon finds an appropriate nomenclature.

104. M. Cousin, in criticising Locke, has some fine remarks on this subject. "The question is, does all error spring from language, and is science nothing else than a well-constructed tongue? No; the causes of our errors are very different, both wider and deeper. Levity, presumption, indolence, precipitation, pride, and thousands of causes influence our judgment. The evils of language may join on to natural causes and aggravate them, but do not constitute them. If you consider them, you will see that the greater part of disputes which appear to be about words, are, at the bottom, disputes about things. Humanity is too earnest to trouble itself and shed its purest blood for words. Wars do not turn on disputes about words; they rise from other quarrels—from quarrels theological and scientific, of which they mistake the depth and importance who resolve them into pure logomachies. Assuredly all science ought to seek a language well constructed; but it is to take the effect for the cause, to suppose that sciences are well constructed because languages are well constructed. The contrary is the truth; the sciences have well-constructed languages when they themselves are well constructed." He illustrates this by mathematics, where the terms are good because the ideas are thoroughly determined; and by such departments as medicine, where we must first employ careful observation and rigid reasoning, and then the appropriate nomenclature will be furnished.

105. But it should be frankly allowed that words, while they are generally a great help to thought, do often hinder it. It may serve some good purposes to consider the evils which arise from the abuse of language. In doing so we shall not dwell on the intentional perversion of words by the sophist, the flatterer, the politician. For these abuses language is not responsible; though it is true that the ambiguous nature of words very much aids the liar and equivocator, and lends some plausibility to the saying that language is rather an instrument for concealing thought.

106. (1.) There is the vagueness of so many phrases. How this should be, the observations we have made on the formation of notions may enable us to understand. In forming abstract terms, we join an aggregate of attributes having a merely superficial and no deep or intimate relation in the nature of things, or more frequently without knowing what are the attributes comprised; and then we make unwarranted assertions regarding that term, saying of one part what is true only of another, or of the whole what is true only of a part. Again, what has been represented (§ 24) as the second essential step in generalization is often performed very imperfectly. We perceive a general resemblance, and we form a class, and we give a name; but meanwhile we have not fixed, except in a loose way, on the points of resemblance, and the phrase goes into circulation carrying its dross with it. Then it is to be taken into account, that in our first generalizations we may fix on the superficial rather than the deeper properties of things. Thus the word money meant originally articles used in exchange, and then was applied to coin; in time it came to have a larger and more scientific meaning; but the ambiguity led the popular mind to identify money with wealth, to conclude that a country must be enriched by increasing its coin, and by passing laws against the exportation of money. It is one of the advantages arising from science, from honest discussion, and the progress of thought generally, that it gives greater precision to language by compelling us to distinguish the diverse things wrapt up in one complex phrase, and to get a separate term for each. It was disputed whether the syllogism was or was not an *invention* of Aristotle, and both parties were right and both wrong according to the use they made of the term. Such discussions led to a distinction being drawn between invention and discovery, the former being confined to the devising of something new, and the latter to the finding out of what before existed: and we now deny that Aristotle invented the syllogism, while we claim for him that he discovered it to be the form to which all reasoning can be reduced. The ancients, and the moderns down to the middle of last century, used the word Sensation to denote both the knowledge and the sensitive feeling got through the senses; Reid drew the distinction between Sensation and Perception; and now, to avoid ambiguity, we employ the phrase Sense-Perception to designate both. It is thus we are getting new notions and new distinctions to supersede or supplement the old; and a permanence is imparted to them by their being stamped with names.

107. (2.) There are different meanings and shades of meaning attached to a word. It is not difficult to understand how this should originate. Every word has a history. If it could speak for itself, instead of being a mere unconscious instrument in the hands of a higher power, it might furnish us with a biography. In doing so, it would have to commence with its genealogy. Many words might furnish us with an older one than the most ancient nobility. Some could point to their ancestry among the Roman patricians; some go back to the Greek gods and demigods; while others ascend to the

Hebrew patriarchs and prophets; not a few boast that they come to us from Paris with the last new fashion; while a considerable class bring with them the broad sense and deep thought of Germany. Our tongue is enriched by these constant importations. But it is to be expected that in such a mixture of emigrants there should be some whose character is very ambiguous. There is the word 'idea,' which has had so many meanings: designating now an image, now an eternal model, now a concept, now an intuitive truth; and the most satisfactory judgment we can pronounce upon one which has had so many *aliases* is, that it should be banished altogether from the commonwealth of philosophy—where it has wrought only mischief—leaving it still a place in common conversation and in poetry. With some, Reason stands for the undefined qualities possessed by man and not by brutes; with others, it signifies much the same as understanding or intelligence, and including the process of reasoning; with others, and especially with the higher metaphysicians of Germany, denoting the capacity which discovers necessary truth immediately, as distinguished from the logical understanding which proceeds discursively,—in this last sense reason and reasoning are contrasted.

108. The perplexity is increased by the circumstance that the phrase has one meaning in one age, and another in another age. Unwilling to offend prejudice, and to give their writings an affected and repulsive aspect, our fresh thinkers retain the old phrase, while they alter the meaning to suit the new aspect of truth to which they would introduce us. "We have resolved to accompany antiquity as far as possible, since we are anxious, so far as it can be done with the pen, to make an alliance between what is old and new in learning. We therefore retain old terms, though we often alter their meaning and definitions, according to that moderate and laudable mode of innovating in civil affairs whereby the condition of things being changed, the usual names are retained; as Tacitus remarks regarding the names of the magistrates which were retained even when the offices were somewhat changed." (Bacon.) This circumstance has bred great confusion. Thus the word Form as distinguished from Matter, has been used in one sense by Aristotle, in another by Bacon, in a third by Kant. From the time of Aristotle to that of David Hume and Kant, to argue 'a priori,' meant to proceed from cause to effect, or from reason to consequent; and to argue 'a posteriori,' to proceed from effect to cause, and from consequent to reason. Since the rise of the Kantian philosophy, by the 'a priori' method is meant proceeding from principles imbedded in the mind and independent of experience.

In the former sense, the famous argument of Samuel Clarke for the existence of God would be called *a priori*, as it proceeds from reason to consequent; but in the latter sense it is partly *a posteriori*, inasmuch as arguing from our idea of space to a being of whom space is an attribute, it proceeds on the fact that man has an idea of space.

109. Little evil would arise from this provided we always distinguished between the meanings. But one use of names, we have seen, is to save us from imaging or remembering all the objects and properties denoted by them. But in the use of ambiguous phrases, especially in abstract discussion, we are apt unconsciously to slide from one meaning to another; and we make an affirmation or denial of a word, using it, in the rapidity of thought, in one sense, whereas the predication would be valid only if we used the phrase in another sense. The ambiguity of the words 'idea,' 'a priori,' 'reason,' has helped to prolong the discussion as to whether there are innate ideas, *a priori* truth, and an intuitive and independent reason in the human mind.

110. The greater number of the words in our language have come down to us from a rude and simple state of society, and they bear the impress of their origin,—resembling in this respect the man who has risen in the world from the lower ranks, and is now admitted, because of his talents and success, to the most polite circles, but who has not been able to shake himself free from the manners of his youth. This, in some aspects, is a disadvantage, as it allows less accuracy of language and thought. To avoid the evil, we very properly bring in terms from the dead classical languages, to express rigidly exact scientific truth. But seen in another light, it is a benefit that our language has sprung from a less artificial condition of things,—just as the most polished circles are all the better of the occasional introduction of persons whose manners, if not so refined, are, at least, more fresh and natural. These old home-born phrases, if not so fitted to express abstract truth, are more effective in evoking genuine and heart-born feeling. I can conceive that some languages, like the manners of some men, might become too artificial. The most perfect tongue is that which has both elements, which seeks to retain the freshness of youth in the midst of the maturity of age.

111. (3.) There are words that mislead us by their associations. Such are phrases which stir up feeling, pleasant or tumultuous. Who can reason calmly when the appeals made deal in such words as home, native land, liberty, independence. Any evil thus arising may be counteracted by the ennobling influence produced by the ideas thus suggested; but it is different when the language raises up passions which agitate the soul as the wind does the ocean, or lusts which pollute it by sinking it in the mire. Again, there are phrases used by our old authors which were not offensive in their day, but are felt by us to be coarse and indelicate. As illustrating the same point, we may refer to the fallacies into which men fall from "usually taking for granted that paronymous (or conjugate) words, *i. e.*, those belonging to each other as the substantive, adjective, verb, &c., of the same roots have a precisely correspondent meaning; which is by no means universally the case." (Whately.) As example we may give art and artful, design and designing, theory and theorist, scheme and schemer. Thus a man is represented as having an art, a design, a theory, or a scheme, and we look upon him as artful, a designer, a theorist, or a schemer. Horne Tooke, the grammarian, argued from the derivation of the word 'true,' that there could be "no such thing as eternal, immutable, everlasting truth." "True," as we now write it, or *trew* as it was formerly written, means simply and merely, that which is trowed. And instead of being a rare commodity on earth, except only in words, there is nothing but truth in the world." "Two persons may contradict each other and yet both speak the truth, for the truth of one person may be opposite to the truth of another. To speak truth may be a vice as well as a virtue."

112. Under this same head we may place the misleading influence of words which now denote mental acts, but which were originally applied to material objects. Thus 'idea' meant originally an image; 'apprehension' and 'conception' are derived from the act of taking hold of a thing; 'understanding' signifies something placed beneath; 'substance,' that which stands beneath; and 'spirit,' in a number of tongues, air or breath. Since mind and body are called substances, some have argued that in addition to the mind and body which we know, and know as having being, permanence, and potency, there must be something standing under them. It is difficult for those whose thoughts are habitually employed about sensible things to conceive of spiritual truths, and the difficulty is increased by the circumstance that the language in which they are expressed was at first materialistic, and is still apt to call up sensible images.

113. (4.) We are led by the advantages which language supplies to use words without inquiring into their meaning. This is in itself the greatest of all the evils, and is the source, directly or indirectly, of most of the others. We have seen that it is one of the main purposes served by symbols, that they render it unnecessary to conceive all that is in the notion, all its objects, and all its marks. But then, just because language so eases thought and labor, we come to give up rigid inquiry and allow words to guide us at their will or caprice. This is one reason why mankind are so apt to follow hereditary or popular beliefs embodied in cherished phrases. "Men," says Locke, "having been accustomed from their cradles to learn words which are easily got and retained, before they knew or had framed the complex ideas to which they were annexed, or which were to be found in the things they were thought to stand for, they usually continue to do so all their lives; and without taking the pains necessary to settle in their minds determined ideas, they use their words for such unsteady and confused notions as they have, contenting themselves with the same words other people use, as if their very sound necessarily carried with it constantly the same meaning. This, though men make a shift with in the ordinary occurrences of life, where they find it necessary to be understood, and, therefore, they make signs till they are so; yet this insignificancy in their words, when they come to reason concerning either their tenets or their interest, manifestly fills their discourse with abundance of empty unintelligible noise and jargon, especially in moral matters, where the words, for the most part, standing for arbitrary and numerous collections of ideas, not regularly and permanently united in their nature, their bare sounds are often only thought on, or at least very obscure and uncertain notions annexed to them."

114. The question arises, how are these evils to be avoided? It is evident that it is not to be done by discarding the use of language—which would be like putting out one's eyes in order to avoid mistakes in vision. Advantage may arise from attending to some such rules as the following :

First. Let us begin with ascertaining the meaning of the word. We may do this by the help of a dictionary ; or by looking to the sense in which it is used by those who intelligently employ it, more specially by resorting to the writings of those who treat expressly of subjects in which it ought to be accurately employed.

115. *Second.* When a word is ambiguous, we should make ourselves acquainted with the various senses in which it is used, not only by the writer whose works we are reading, but those in which others, or in which we ourselves, have been accustomed to employ it. If we have not before us the various senses and the difference between them, we shall ever be tempted to slide from the one to the other without knowing it. Thus, in mental philosophy, we must never lose sight of the various senses in which the phrases 'idea,' 'a priori,' 'a posteriori,' 'experience,' 'form' and 'matter,' 'subject' and 'object,' 'conditioned' and 'unconditioned,' are employed. If we neglect this, we are certain to be led astray by the errors which lurk beneath these phrases, all of which have been used in different senses and been the vehicles of false doctrines.

116. *Third.* We must be at pains to settle the precise notion which the word stands for. This implies much more than a dictionary understanding of it. It requires that we go back to the notion in the mind. For every term stands primarily for an apprehension of the mind ; that apprehension must, no doubt, be of objects, but it is of objects apprehended, and so we must look first at the apprehension, and then compare it with the things. This is a counsel frequently pressed by Locke. "A man should take care to use no word without a signification, no name without an idea for which he makes it stand. This rule will not seem altogether needless, to any one who will take the pains to recollect how often he has met with such words as instinct, sympathy, antipathy, &c., in the discourse of others, so made use of as he might easily conclude that those that used them had no ideas in their mind to which they applied them; but spoke them only as sounds, which usually served instead of reasons, on the like occasions. Not but that these words, and the like, have very proper significations in which they may be used, but there being no natural connexion between any words and any ideas, these and any others may be learned by rote and pronounced or writ by men who have no ideas in their minds to which they have annexed them, and for which they make them stand; which is necessary they should, if men would speak intelligibly even to themselves." "Justice is a word in every man's mouth, but most commonly with a very undetermined, loose signification, which will always be so, unless a man has in his mind a distinct comprehension of the component parts that complex idea consists of: and if it be decomposed, must be able to resolve still on, till he at last comes to the simple ideas that make it up; and unless this be done a man makes an ill use of the word; let it be justice, for example, or any other. I do not say a man need stand to recollect and make this analysis at large, every time the word justice comes in his way; but this at least is necessary, that he have so examined the signification of that name, and settled the idea in all its parts in his mind, that he can do it when he pleases."

117. *Fourth.*—Let us observe whether the notions are Singulars, or Abstracts, or Universals. We are reading, let me suppose, of beauty, and we are anxious to have clear ideas on the subject. Let us first inquire what sort of notion is denoted by the word. We easily and at once discover that it is an Abstract notion, and therefore we do not for one instant suppose that it has, or can have, a separate existence. We are not, on the other hand, rashly to conclude that it has no existence. It is a reality, but a reality in objects; and we are led to look to objects and inquire what it is in them that we designate by this name.

Or the word we have occasion to employ is a General one. We have now to inquire what is the class of objects connoted by it, and what the common qualities in respect of which they are grouped. The word used, I shall suppose, is 'instinctive;' it is said of such an action that it is 'instinctive.' We proceed on the idea that it points to a reality; but we do not suppose that it is a reality distinct from the beings possessing it: we look for it in the living beings endowed with it, and we proceed to inquire what it is, whether it is a single property or, as is more probable, a number of properties adapted to each other and tending to one end.

When the notion is what I have called a Generalized Concrete one, we are to bear in mind that we cannot expect to exhaust all the properties of the objects embraced in the class. It was foolish and vain to seek, as Socrates seems to have done, for some one thing as constituting the τὸ ὂν of a class notion, say the τὸ καλὸν; or as the schoolmen did, to specify the essence of every universal, as, for instance, of man.

118. It is of great moment to take these cautions with us in all our higher thinking, in which we are ever tempted to look upon abstractions as independent wholes. The ancient Greek philosophers often gave a separate existence to the abstractions fashioned by them. Thus the Eleatics, and Plato after them, were accustomed to discuss the nature of τὸ ὄν, or being, as if it were a distinct substance like mind or body. We have fallen into a like mistake in modern times. We speak very properly of the faculties of the mind, such as the memory, the imagination, and judgment ; but then we are led to think and write about them as if they were acting entities, whereas they are merely capacities of the thinking mind. We find ethical writers speaking of virtue as if it were something separate from and above the virtuous mind ; whereas it is a mere attribute of virtuous agents, from which it cannot be separated except in mental abstraction. Some write about gravitation as if it had an independent existence, whereas it is a mere property of matter having no existence separate from individual bodies. Again, general terms are apt to be regarded as singulars. Men speak and reason as if general phrases pointed to some one existence, whereas they merely connote a class of things having one or more points of resemblance. Some discourse about the laws of nature, as if they were something different from the objects in the universe, whereas they are generalizations of the modes in which the objects operate. Having begun with this blunder in thought, there are some who go a step farther and make the laws of nature a substitute for Deity. They have first given them an existence separate from God's works, and having got such a convenient mode of accounting for these works, they feel as if nature could work without God altogether. We are reminded of an analogous error. We employ the word ' nature ' as a convenient one to denote the whole knowable creation as it comes from God's hands. But we forget that the phrase is merely a generic one, and then are led to talk of nature as having an existence separate from the combined works of God. Having given it an independent existence we end by deifying it—I fear nature is the only God worshipped by many of the votaries of physical science in our day.

119. *Fifth.*—We must carefully consider the things from which the notions have been formed. I believe, indeed, that we ought first to look to the notions, for words stand primarily for apprehensions of the mind. But apprehensions, so far as they profess to be drawn from things, must conform to them, and in order to see whether our notions are accurate and adequate, we must ever compare them with the things from which they are derived. We have seen that the great English metaphysician has done signal service to philosophy by insisting that we always rise from terms to the ideas they stand for. But another English philosopher has, if possible, conferred a greater benefit by requiring that we should ever go beyond notions to things. Bacon complains, I believe justly, of the ancient Greek philosophers and of the scholastic logicians, that they looked at names which had no corresponding objects, or at notions abstracted from things; that their very definitions consist of words, and "verba gignunt verba. Verba notionum tesseræ sunt, quare si notiones ipsæ (quæ verborum animæ sunt) male et varie abstrahantur tota fabrica corruit." And so he recommends the observation of things by a careful induction as the means of attaining truth and certainty; and in doing so has given a nobler contribution to the science of Logic, in the enlarged sense of the term, than any other except Aristotle.

LAWS OF THOUGHT INVOLVED IN THE USE OF SIGNS.

120. *First Law.*—Every Term stands for a Notion, which must be either a Singular Concrete, an Abstract, or a Universal. We should accustom ourselves, in thinking, to look more to the notion than the phraseology, and we should ever be ready to translate our words into thoughts. But if the analysis which we have given of notions be correct, these terms when turned into notions will be found to be one or other of our threefold division : they will be Percepts or of single things thought of in the Concrete ; or Abstracts, that is of qualities ; or Concepts, that is of a class of objects joined by common qualities. Now it is often of great moment in discussing a complicated subject, that we should know precisely to which of these classes the notion which we are using belongs, and that we should understand it, and use it accordingly. If we neglect this, if we employ, for example, abstract and general terms as if they were singulars, or treat abstract and general terms as if they had no sort of reality, we shall find ourselves involved first in inextricable confusion, and then in positive error.

121. *Second Law.*—We can predicate of the Sign only what might be predicated of the Notion. We have seen that after we have denoted a notion by a sign we can judge and reason about the sign without thinking of all that is signified by it. But we must not allow ourselves for one moment to suppose that the sign has acquired any new power not found in that which it stands for, or that we are at liberty to affirm or deny of it what we would not affirm or deny of the notion itself provided it stood fairly before us. If A stands for a square number, we are not allowed to predicate of it what we could not predicate of the square number itself, say that it is a virtue. If B stands for a moral quality, say justice, we are not to be allowed to affirm of it what could not be affirmed of justice, say that it has four sides. The sign is still a sign, a sign of what it was made to stand for.

122. *Third Law.*—We may demand at any time, that the Notion should be substituted for the Sign. As we are always at liberty to do so, so we should actually do so from time to time, in order to determine whether we are or are not making a proper predication.. In abstruse discussion and in perplexing ratiocination, we are apt to lose sight of the signification, or at least of the precise signification, of the language we employ. But as we do so we are ever liable to make affirmations or denials which we should never make of the ideas denoted by the words. Principal Campbell inquires: "What is the cause that nonsense so often escapes being detected both by the writer and reader?" The cause, I believe, is to be found mainly in this, that we are ever making assertions as to the sign, taking a loose view of what it signifies. Thus our forefathers reasoned that as money is wealth, so wealth might be increased by passing restrictive laws to keep money from leaving the country. The fallacy is seen at once when we properly define and studiously comprehend what the phrases money and wealth stand for. From the causes now referred to, mainly proceed the endless logomachies to be found in controversy of every kind. We shall often find that we have only to retranslate the word into the notion, and then compare the notion with the thing, to discover that the propositions which men utter with such gravity, or such confidence, are altogether meaningless, and that the sophistry which was deceiving us, is thus stript of its plausibilities. Every one will be inclined to allow that we should be careful to follow this rule when we are apt to run into extreme positions, or are penetrating into profound depths or vast heights. But in fact, it is equally needful to do so, when we are using familiar phrases, which we fancy we understand fully because we have been employing them daily from our childhood. As Newton is said to have risen to his great discovery by narrowly inquiring into so commonplace a fact as the fall of an apple, so the detection of wide-spread fallacies and the discovery of important truth are ofttimes made by instituting a sifting inquiry into the real signification of a phrase, which without being questioned by any one, has passed current from mouth to mouth for long ages.

III.—CLASSES IN NATURE.

123. These become aids and guides to the mind in its generalizations. I speak of them as aids, for the mind by its own internal power can form genera without any special reference to natural groupings. It must always, indeed, have some supposed attribute to bind the objects together, and act as ground of the arrangement. But then it can fix on any one attribute and form a class composed of all the objects which possess it. Every thing may be arranged in as many classes, actual or potential, as it possesses qualities. The same man may, in respect of his country, be an Englishman or an American ; of his religion, a Catholic or a Protestant ; of his race, a Celt or a Saxon ; of his profession, a lawyer or a physician ; of his domestic condition a bachelor, or married ; of his politics, a conservatist or a liberal ; of his knowledge, a scholar or an ignoramus. Looking to any given company of men, women, and children, we might arrange them in a great number of ways : according to their native country or county ; according to their sex, age, weight, strength, mental capacities, education, business in life, character, creed ; nay, according to such insignificant qualities as the color of their hair or eyes, or their Christian names. Wherever, in short there is a property which more than one person possess or are supposed to possess, we have a ground for a classification which may be expressed by a generic term. The classes which man may form cannot be said to be infinite, but they are indefinite ; no limits can be set to them. There is a manifest advantage in all this ;

for we can arrange the objects we meet with, now in this way and now in that way, according to the end we have in view at the time.

124. But so far as natural and especially organic objects are concerned, there are groupings formed which men should notice, and which have an existence whether they notice them or no. In the study of nature we are constantly made to feel that we have not to form or create classes ; the classes are already formed for us, and all we have to do is simply to observe them. And if we would construct any thing like a complete classification of natural objects, it is imperative on us to attend to the natural groupings. An arrangement which overlooks this will turn out to be incomplete, and incapable of serving any practical purpose ; and however ingeniously formed will be characterized as artificial, even when not denounced as arbitrary and capricious. The Creator has so constructed and disposed his works that there are facilities for forming classes, and it is the business of the naturalist to discover and follow the natural order. So far as he gets hold of it his classifications will be natural, and useful for the accomplishment of an immense number and variety of purposes, scientific and practical.

125. We have shown (*Method of Divine Government*, B. II., C. I., § 4. and *Typical Forms and Special Ends in Creation*), that there is an order running through all nature in respect of such qualities as Number, Time, and Form. (1.) *Number*. The laws of physics and of chemistry, etc., are expressed in quantities. The law of gravitation is, that all matter attracts other matter inversely according to the square of the distance; and all chemical compositions and decompositions take place according to numerical rule. (2.) *Time*. All the leading events in the earth and heavens run in periods : there are days and months and seasons and years, and *magni anni*. (3.) *Form*. The heavenly bodies have spheroidal shapes ; minerals crystallize geometrically with fixed angles and proportions : and every animal and plant and every organ of the animal and plant, has a typical form which it tends to assume.

126. We are thus introduced to those classes which have been called Kinds by some logicians. In these the possession of one characteristic mark is a sign of a number of others. The botanist has seized on a classification of this kind. The grand division of plants is into acotyledons, monocotyledons, and dicotyledons. This is a distinction of Kinds, and the mark fixed on becomes the sign of others. Thus monocotyledons grow from within and their leaves are parallel-veined, whereas dicotyledons grow from without by adding rings and have netted veins. In the same way in the approved classifications of zoology, the possession of one mark becomes a sign of others. Thus certain animals are called mammals because they suckle their young ; but all these are found besides to be warm-blooded, and to have four compartments in the heart. How different are these from artificial classes, as suppose we were to divide plants according to their height, or animals according to their color. Every one sees how arbitrary, in short how unnatural, such an arrangement would be. It would separate plants from each other which are most closely allied, and might put in one group bird and fish, man and brute, while it separated an animal from its mate or from its offspring.

127. "There are some classes the things contained in which differ from other things only in certain particulars which may be numbered ; while others differ in more than can be numbered, more even than we need ever expect to know. Some classes have little or nothing in common to characterize them by, except precisely what is connoted by the name: white things, for example, are not distinguished by any common properties except whiteness: or if they are, it is only by such as are in some way dependent upon, or connected with whiteness. But a hundred generations have not exhausted the common properties of animals or of plants, of sulphur or of phosphorus ; nor do we suppose them to be exhaustible, but proceed to new observations and experiments, in the full confidence of discovering new properties which were by no means implied in those we previously knew." "There is no impropriety in saying that of these two classifications, the one answers to a much more radical distinction in the things themselves than the other does, etc." (Mill's *Logic*, B. I., C. VII.)

128. These groupings of nature, while they are a help, are at the same time a rule in the formation of classes. They assist, but they also control mankind in the construction and use of their general notions. Things come to be arranged by practical observation and by science in a certain way ; a corresponding nomenclature is devised, and all men must accommodate themselves to it. Such divisions of time as into days and years and seasons, of material objects into mineral, plant, and animal, of the heavenly bodies into star, planet, comet, and meteor, come to be universally adopted, and all persons must proceed upon them ; while science is every year adding newly-discovered laws, which become known first to the learned and then descend as a heritage to the people. The concepts thus formed on distinctions in nature, have a reality above other concepts. Such a concept as 'white-colored,' has, no doubt, a sort of reality in the nature of things—it has a reality in the white color possessed by all the objects in the class, say lilies and snow. But such concepts as Rosaceæ and Cruciferæ, as Crustaceæ and Foraminiferæ, have a deeper signification—the class has a reality in the divinely appointed order of things. It is the same with such generic notions as beautiful, good, holy—they denote primarily one quality, but they imply other qualities associated with it and numberless affinities. This was one of the truths pointed at, but never accurately expressed in, the ideal theory of Plato and the medieval doctrine of realism. Concepts of this description have a place in the very nature of things and in their ramified connections. But while this holds good of certain concepts, it is not true of all ; and even in regard to those of which it is true, the reality is, after all, in the individual things and their mutual relations, and not in a mere idea in the mind of the person contemplating them.

REALISM, NOMINALISM, AND CONCEPTUALISM.

129. In the *Eisagoge* of Porphyry there occurs the following statement: "I omit to speak about genera and species as to whether they subsist (in the nature of things) or in mere conceptions only; whether also, if subsistent, they are bodies or incorporeal, or whether they are separate from or in sensibles and subsist about these." Boethius (6th *Cent.*) commented on this passage and declared: "non est dubium quin vere sint." "Sunt autem in rebus omnibus conglutinatæ et quodam modo conjunctæ atque compactæ." This came to be the general and the orthodox opinion of the early scholastic teachers. But as curious youths mused on this cautious passage of Porphyry with the comment of Boethius upon it, we can conceive that some would be tempted to form an independent opinion on so complicated a subject. This seems to have been the case with Roscellinus, a native of Brittany, who flourished in the eleventh century. Unfortunately we have no writings of Roscellinus, and we have to gather his opinions from the statements of his opponents, particularly Anselm. He is represented as maintaining that genera and species had no true existence—that they were nothing but words (*flatus vocis*), and this doctrine was denounced as inconsistent with the higher doctrines of religion, particularly the doctrine of the Trinity. We have now, then, an expounder of Nominalism as opposed to Realism. At a little later date appeared the illustrious Abelard, who opposed with great acuteness the systems both of the Realists and the Nominalists, pointing out the difficulties in which the former are involved when they maintained that universals are realities different from individual things, and showing the insufficiency of the theory of the latter. His own opinion is regarded by some as Conceptualism—it is at least an anticipation of Conceptualism. The following is M. Cousin's account of it: "There exists nothing but individuals, but none of these individuals is, in itself, either genus or species, but the individuals have resemblances which the mind can perceive, and these resemblances considered alone and abstraction being made of their differences, form classes more or less comprehensive which they call genus or species. Species and genus are then the real products of the mind; and they are not words, although words express them; nor are they things without or within the individuals—they are conceptions. Hence the intermediate system named Conceptualism." (*Fragmens*). We have now the three possible systems contending with each other. Realism was the prevailing doctrine throughout the Middle Ages, and was defended with great zeal and ability by Albert of Cologne (*Albertus Magnus*), and Thomas Aquinas (*Doctor Angelicus*). Opposed to Thomas the Dominican was John Duns Scotus (*Doctor Subtilis*) the Franciscan. Like Thomas he was a Realist, but he maintained that the universal existed in individuals not really, but formally (*formaliter*). William Occam (*Doctor Invincibilis*) a disciple of Scotus, is usually regarded as a Nominalist, but Dr. Mansel declares that he is a Conceptualist like Abelard. In modern times it is difficult to find a genuine Realist, but we have one in Harris, the author of Hermes. Adhering to the Nominalist theory we have Hobbes, Berkeley, Hume and Whately; and among numerous Conceptualists we may mention Locke, Reid, Kant, Brown, and Whewell.

130. The controversy has been characterized throughout by great confusion of thought. The extensive survey we have taken of the Notion and of Language should enable us to discover the truth and the error in each of the systems.

Realism errs by excess. It errs when it ascribes to the universal an existence independent of singulars or distinct from them. Plato held that Ideas had an existence in or before the Divine Mind from all eternity. He was met by Aristotle, who showed that they had no existence except in the individuals. The medieval doctrine of the reality in universals was a modification of the Platonic doctrine. In both there is a tendency to mysticism, and a disposition to hypostasize the conceptions of the mind. Yet the system has noticed certain important truths. First the mind has a tendency to rise beyond the particular to the general, and to reduce multiplicity to unity. Then all organisms, all plants and animals, tend to assume a typical form. The individuals all die, showing how perishing they are, but the genus and species survive. The flowers of last summer are all faded, but in the coming summer flowers of the same form will spring up. Then all the powers of nature act according to laws imposed on them, and amidst the flux of things these laws are permanent. Still more important, we find, amidst the imperfections and sins of humanity, the moral law of God abideth forever.

131. *Nominalism* errs by defect. It forgets that there must be grouping of objects by the mind in order to the introduction of a common term, and an apprehension of the grouping in order to an intelligent use of the term. It forgets that the mind can form an image of a class of objects, inadequate, but still sufficient in most cases to enable it to think about them. It overlooks the important circumstance that in nature there are laws and types ordained by the Being who formed the objects themselves. The truth contained in nominalism is, that words greatly aid the mind in thinking, and enable it to conduct its cogitations much farther than it otherwise could.

132. *Conceptualism* has often taken a wrong form. It does so when it regards the conception combining the objects as an idea in the sense of image. This was the mistake of Locke, when he says that in forming our idea of man we leave out of the complex idea that which is peculiar to each of the individuals, and retain only what is common to all. (See § 79.) Again it errs when it overlooks or denies the utility, in some cases the necessity, of signs to enable us to conduct our thinking. And Conceptualists have often, in looking at the idea, forgot that there is an actual order among the things on which the idea is founded. But if it avoids these mistakes and oversights, which are not parts of the doctrine properly understood, conceptualism is the true theory. For in general notions, the essential element is the grouping by the mind of objects by common properties, and putting in the group all objects possessing the properties.

PART SECOND.

JUDGMENT.

1. JUDGMENT is defined by logicians "as the comparing together in the mind two of the notions or ideas which are the objects of apprehension, and pronouncing that they agree or disagree." But this definition can be accepted only when we understand by notions, not mental states as such, but objects apprehended. When we say "Alexander the Great was ambitious," we are comparing "Alexander the Great" and "ambitious," and not mere ideas of the mind—it being always presupposed that the objects are previously apprehended by us. A Proposition is a Judgment expressed in words, and in it we compare two Terms, so called because they are the *termini* (boundaries) of the proposition.

CATEGORICAL PROPOSITIONS.

2. Judgment is psychologically one act of the mind, but is of a concrete nature, and we analyze it into three elements, two notions, and the declaration of their agreement or disagreement. That notion which we seek primarily to compare is called the Subject; that with which we compare it, the Predicate; and the determination of the agreement or disagreement, the Copula. The Judgment may be expressed in three words, or in a number of words, or even in one word. When we say "selfishness is hateful," we have subject, copula, and predicate, each in one word. But there are tongues in which the judgment can be expressed in one word, as *amat;* which, when we wish to bring out each of the parts we analyze and say, *ille est amans*, he is loving. Active verbs in a sentence commonly express both copula and predicate; thus, when we say "the horse neighs," the word 'neighs' contains both predicate and predication, and when expanded takes the form "the horse is neighing." In order to determine what are the terms, we must look, not to the mere words, which may differ in different languages and even in the same language in expressing the same idea, but to the notions. When it is said that "it is a true saying and worthy of all acceptation, that Jesus Christ came into the world to save sinners," the two terms, as ascertained from the two notions, are "Jesus Christ coming into the world to save sinners" and "a true saying and worthy of all acceptation;" these are the things compared in the mind, and in respect of which we predicate their agreement.

3. The copula is usually expressed by logicians by the present tense of the verb 'to be,' by 'is,' or 'is not,' (or 'are' and 'are not.') But we are not to understand 'is' in such a connection, as being the substantive verb—the substantive verb in the Latin form, *est*, contains subject, copula, and predicate, meaning "he is existing." The copula is an abstract, expressing neither less nor more than the agreement or disagreement. Every thing else in a proposition is to be regarded as part of the subject or of the predicate. The element of time, when it is involved in a judgment, is not to be attached to the copula. When we say "Napoleon Bonaparte was unfortunate in 1815," the notions compared are "Napoleon in 1815" and "unfortunate," and it is on comparing these that we declare their agreement; if we were speaking of "Napoleon in 1808," we should have to declare that it disagreed with "unfortunate."

4. It is thus that most logicians do now dispose of what are called Modals, that is, propositions in which we make a predication, not absolutely, but after a mode. Thus, when it is said that "Brutus killed Cæsar justly," we are not to understand the predicate as being "the killer of Cæsar," but "the just killer of Cæsar."

5. The QUALITY (ποιότης) of a proposition, that which makes it to be a proposition or a judgment, is its predication, its affirming or denying an agreement or disagreement between the terms. In respect of Quality, all propositions are either Affirmative or Negative—they either affirm or deny the agreement of the subject and predicate.

6. The predicate may be affirmed or denied either of the whole or part of the subject. When it is predicated of the whole, the proposition is said to be Universal; when not of the whole, it is said to be Particular (ἐν μέρει). This division of propositions is said to be made in respect of their QUANTITY, that is, the extent of the predication. When it is said "all poets are men of genius," the proposition is universal, the affirmation is made of all poets. When it is said "some poets have not common sense," the assertion is made only of a part of the class. Such phrases as "every one" and "all" in affirmative propositions, and "no," "no one," and "none" in negative propositions, are the signs of universality. The sign of particularity is "some" in the sense of "some at least," —we may not know how much or how many.

7. The word "all" is ambiguous. It may mean "every one," every one of a class, as when we say "all books are meant to be read." It may also mean all collectively, meaning the whole class, as "all the books constitute the library." In this latter sense, the term is singular-abstract. (See § 48). In both senses the proposition is reckoned Universal. The word "some" is also ambiguous.

It may signify "some, not all," "some at most;" as when we say "some lawyers are not greedy," implying that there are some who are. It may mean "some-certain," as when it is said that "some sciences are classificatory," pointing to mineralogy, botany, and zoology. In Logic "some," as the sign of particularity, signifies "some at least;" it may be only one, or it may even be all, provided we do not declare it to be all.

8. In order to determine the quantity of a proposition, we must look, it is evident, to the subject. In many sentences the quantity is not indicated by the language, but it must always be understood in thought. When it is said that "men have the power of speech," we mean "all men," and not merely "some men." But when it is said that "books are necessary to a library," we mean not "all books," but "some books." Terms in which the quantity is not indicated by the language are called "indefinite" or "indesignate" (Hamilton).

9. Combining these cross-divisions, we have a fourfold division of propositions:

Universal Affirmative	denoted by	A.
Universal Negative	"	E.
Particular Affirmative	"	I.
Particular Negative	"	O.

Asserit A, negat E, verum generaliter ambo.
Asserit I, negat O, sed particulariter ambo.

10. This may be the proper place for explaining what is meant by the Distribution of Terms in a proposition. A term is said to be distributed when it is used for all its significates. When it is said "reptiles are cold-blooded," the general term "reptiles" is distributed—it includes all and every reptile. But when it is said that "food is necessary to life," the general term "food" is not distributed, for it does not mean every kind of food, but food of some kind. Singular Terms and Abstracts are always to be reckoned as distributed. When it is said

"Shakespeare is the greatest poet that ever lived," Shakespeare is to be taken for the man, for the man as a whole—we do not make the affirmation of some Shakespeare, or Shakespeare in part; and the proposition is regarded as universal, A, by logicians. It is the same with abstracts proper, as "pride goeth before destruction," meaning, not "some pride," but the one thing "pride." It is always to be kept in mind, indeed, that abstracts may become common terms (see § 49), as when we talk of various kinds of pride, as pride of intellect, pride of life; in such we are to ascertain whether the term is distributed or not, as we do in the case of any other general term.

11. From the account now given, it is clear that in all Universal propositions, A and E, the Subject is distributed, and that in all particular propositions, I and O, it is undistributed. As to the Predicate, it is to be regarded as distributed in all negative propositions. When we say "no brute is immortal," "some men are not misers," we exclude brutes from the whole class of immortals, and certain men from the whole class of misers. When the Predicate is a general notion, it is not to be understood as distributed in affirmative propositions. When it is said that "men are mortal," the term mortal is not taken for all its significates; we cannot say "all mortals are men." But it is of importance to remark (the significance of it will come out as we advance) that as singular and abstract terms are distributed and regarded as universals, so the predicates which are formed by such are always to be regarded as distributed. In the propositions "Homer was the author of the Iliad" and the "Iliad was the greatest of Greek poems," the terms "author of the Iliad," and "the greatest of Greek poems," are taken in all their extent.

12. The question is much discussed, what are the relations between the objects compared in a judgment. The proper answer is that they may be as many and varied as the relations which can be discovered between things by the mind of man. What is the number and what the nature of these relations, is a question to be settled—if it can be settled—by physics or metaphysics, and not by logic. The varied relations are all involved in those acts in which we compare single objects with each other. Judgments in regard to individual things must evidently be the first formed by the mind—they must precede the formation of concepts, for it is by resemblance between individuals in respect of some quality that we are able to gather them into classes. Such judgments have been called Psychological by Dr. Mansel, to distinguish them from Logical. For logical purposes, that is in the discursive comparison of notions, judgments may be regarded as of two kinds.

13. N.B. The relations which the mind can discover have been variously classified by philosophers. In the *Intuitions of the Mind,* (P. II., b. iii.), the human intellect is represented as capable of perceiving the relations of (1) Identity, that is, that the same is the same observed at different times and in different circumstances; (2) Whole and Parts (Comprehension, Abstraction, Analysis, Synthesis); (3) Space (Extension, Figure); (4) Time; (5) Quantity (Less or More); (6) Resemblance (Classification); (7) Active Property; (8) Cause and Effect. These may all be noticed in the relation of individual things. But for logical ends the relations may be considered as two.

14. *First.* There are Equivalent Propositions, or Equipollent Propositions—to use a phrase of the old logicians somewhat modified. Here the agreement of the terms is one of identity or equality. In all such the subject may take the place of the predicate, and the predicate the place of the subject without any change. Under this head should be placed all those cases in which both the notions compared are Singulars or Abstracts, as "Milton was the author of Paradise Lost," "Romulus was the founder of Rome." These propositions being given, we can say "The author of Paradise Lost was Milton," "The founder of Rome was Romulus." To this class belong arithmetical and geometrical propositions as $3 + 3 = 6$. Here the terms are abstracts, and we can say $6 = 3 + 3$. It is of importance to observe that to this class belong all definitions, as "Logic is the science of the laws of discursive thought," Natural History is the science of the classification of animals and plants." In these propositions the terms are Abstracts, neither Percepts on the one hand, nor Concepts on the other; and we can convert simply, and say "the science of the Laws of discursive thought is Logic" and "the science of the laws of the classification of animals and plants is Natural History." (See P. I., § 73.) In all such, neither term has any claim in itself to be regarded as subject or as predicate. That is the subject which is primarily before the mind of the speaker to be compared with something else, and that is the predicate with which it is compared; and the speaker or writer may have either term primarily in his thoughts, or now he may have one and now the other.

15. *Second.* There are propositions in which the agreement is one of joint Comprehension and Extension. In all such it will be found that one of the notions is a concept, or that both are so. Take the proposition "Longfellow is a poet." Here the subject is a Percept, and the predicate a Concept. The proposition may be interpreted in one or other of two ways: in Comprehension, meaning that "Longfellow has the attribute of writing poetry;" or in Extension, meaning that "he is in the class of poets." Or we may take a case in which both terms are Concepts, as "Crocodiles are reptiles;" which may be interpreted "the class crocodiles possess the attributes of reptiles;" or, "the class crocodiles are in the class reptiles." It has often been disputed whether propositions are to be understood in Comprehension or Extension. The proper account is that in those we are now speaking of they are to be understood in both. I believe, indeed, that in the greater number of propositions, in particular in all propositions in which the predicate is a verb, the uppermost thought is in Comprehension: when we say "men think," we mean that they are in the exercise of thinking. But as an attribute possessed by objects may always be a bond to unite them into a class, so we may interpret the proposition in Extension also, and say "men are among the class of thinking beings." And in many propositions the uppermost thought is in Extension. When we say "the crocodile is a reptile," our primary intention may be to indicate that it is in the class. But as Extension always implies Comprehension, that is, a class always implies a quality to bring the objects into the unity of a concept, so we may always interpret the proposition in Comprehension likewise, and say "the crocodile has the attributes of reptiles."

16. The distinction between these two classes is of great logical importance. It was noticed by Aristotle who divided propositions into Convertible and Unconvertible, and appears in the present day in the distinction drawn by Archbishop Thomson between Substitutive and Attributive Judgments. We have seen that in the former class we can at once put the subject in the place of the predicate, and the predicate in the room of the subject. In the other we cannot do so without changing the predicate; thus in the Attributive Judgment "all men think," we cannot convert simply, and affirm "all thinking beings are men." It has not been noticed that in the first class both notions are Percepts or Abstracts, and that in the second the predicate is a Concept.

17. In the second class there is a real difference between the subject and the predicate, whereby the one comes primarily and the other secondarily in the order of thought. We may say for poetical effect "sweet is the breath of morn," but the natural order in thought is "the breath of morn is sweet." The rationale is, that in predication we ascribe an attribute to an object, or we place it in a class ; and in both the predicate must be more extensive and less comprehensive than the subject. This is the the rule at least for affirmative propositions, that the subject is the more comprehensive and less extensive.

18. Certain negative propositions seem to be exceptions. Thus when we say "all Greeks were not Athenians," the subject is more extensive than the predicate. But the proposition is not a universal negative, E : we do not say of every one of the Greeks that they were not Athenians, or that no Greek was an Athenian ; but that "some Greeks were not Athenians." But then even in this form the subject is the more extensive. But is not the proposition in thought "some Greeks were Not-Athenians," in which we constitute a class of all persons Not-Athenians, which is more extensive than Greeks?

19. It is disputed what we are to make of those propositions in which the predicate is a general notion distributed, *e. g.*, "all men are all rational beings." It is clear that when we say simply "all men are rational," we mean that every one man, every one in the class man, is in the class rational. But if we have farther found that every rational being is in the class man, we are entitled to say "all men are all rational." But what do we mean when we say so? The terms, it appears to us, are no longer general, standing for each and every one of a class ; we do not mean "every one man = all rational," nor "every one man = every rational." The word "all" does not now mean "every one," but the whole collectively (see § 48). The meaning in fact now is, "the whole class men = the whole class rational." If so, the terms are not General, applicable to each and every one of an indefinite number, but Singular, with a process of Abstraction involved. To take one other example. The mathematician demonstrates that "equilateral triangles are equiangular," meaning that every one equilateral triangle is so. He also demonstrates that "equiangular triangles are equilateral." He can now say "the whole class of equilateral triangles is equal in extent to the whole class of equilateral," and the terms are Singular Abstracts, and the propositions Convertible, Substitutive, Equivalent or Equipollent.

20. We have called attention (§ 9) to the fourfold division of propositions A, E, I, O. But we have now seen that there is a class of Universal Affirmative propositions in which the predicate is distributed. To distinguish them from A, in which the predicate is not distributed, it is proposed to designate them by the vowel U (Hamilton), or A^2 (Spalding), which would represent that class of propositions in which the terms are Singulars or Abstracts, and Convertible.

21. According to Aristotle, every proposition declares a genus (νένος), or a property (ἴδιον), or a definition (ὅρος), or accident (συμβεβηκός), of the subject. Genus denotes a part or attribute belonging to the subject, but also to other subjects, as "mammals are vertebrates," where the predicate applies to other subjects as well. A property belongs invariably to the subject, but without being the mark which explains its nature, as that "mammals are warm-blooded." Definition is an attribute or set of attributes explaining the very nature of the subject, as that mammals suckle their young. Accident is an attribute belonging to the subject, but which might be conceivably separated from it, as that mammals are found in America. This makes the predicables four in number. Porphyry has five Predicables, genus, species, proprium, differentia, and accident, leaving out definition and adding species (εἶδος) and differentia (διαφορὰ). Species is the whole essence of its subject. Differentia is that attribute or set of attributes by which a species is distinguished from other species of its genus.

Some of these distinctions are of great importance, as that between genus and species (P. I., § 35); and that between definition and proprium, or, as Porphyry makes it, between differentia and proprium. In species and differentia, *e. g.*, "mammals suckle their young," the subject and predicate are convertible or equivalent or coextensive. In proprium, *e. g.*, that "mammals are warm-blooded," the terms are not convertible, for there are warm-blooded animals which are not mammals. The distinction between differentia and proprium is valuable as showing that when we have fixed on the differentia of a class, we may often find other attributes conjoined with it which may be called propria. This is the case with those classes which are called Kinds (see P. I., § 126). It is difficult, however, in some circumstances, to determine what is differentia and what is property. Under one view, that is, to the sailor, polarity would be the differentia of the magnet, while under another aspect, "to those manufacturers who employ magnets for the purpose of more expeditiously picking up small bits of iron and for shielding their faces from the noxious steel-dust in the grinding of needles, the attracting power of the magnet is the essential point." (Whately.) It is extremely difficult to carry out these distinctions thoroughly and consistently. We cannot tell what is the whole essence of any subject; all that we can do is to specify one or more of the determining attributes of a species. Nor can we say in all circumstances what is an accident as distinguished from a property, say, *e. g.*, whether that it lives on the earth is the property or accident of a mammal. The distinction adopted in the text between Equivalent propositions in which the terms are coextensive and interchangeable, and Attributive propositions in which the relation is one of joint comprehension and extension and in which the predicate is undistributed, seems to be the important one for logical ends.

22. Hamilton maintains that the predicate should always be quantified, that is, declared to be either particular or universal; that we should say logically, "all men = some fallible." He argues this on the ground that whatever is contained implicitly in spontaneous thought should be unfolded explicitly in logical forms. We admit the principle, but we deny that it requires the quantification of the predicate in affirmative propositions. In the great majority of affirmative propositions, the predication is made in comprehension rather than extension. When we say "the bird sings," we are attributing a quality to the bird, and we are not determining in thought whether there are or are not other creatures that sing

When we say "man reasons," we are ascribing a property to him probably without settling whether there are or are not other beings who reason; and so the logician is not required to put the proposition either in the form "all men = some reasoning beings," or "all men = all reasoning beings." And this may be the proper place for stating that there is no appropriateness in using the sign of equality, =, which has a definite meaning in mathematics, to express the connection of the notions in attributive propositions in which the relation is one of comprehension and extension and not of mere equality.

23. Carrying out his doctrine of the thorough quantification of the predicate in all propositions, Sir W. Hamilton gives the following Table of Judgments:

A All plants grow.
E No right action is inexpedient.
I Some muscles are without our volition.
O Some plants do not grow in the tropics.
U Common salt is chloride of sodium.
Y Some stars are all the planets.
η No Frenchman is some German.
ω Some trees (oaks) are not some trees (elms).

The two marked by the Greek letters are criticised by Thomson and rejected on the ground that while they are conceivable cases of negative predication they are not actual—we would add in spontaneous thought. Thus η has the resemblance, not the power of denial; it denies nothing, and decides nothing. Y should also be discarded on the ground that it is never uttered by us in spontaneous thought, in which we say instead "all the planets are stars," which is A. Rejecting these three forms on these special grounds, we farther decline to give them a separate place in the Table of Judgments, on the general ground that in spontaneous thought the predicate is not quantified in all or even in most judgments. We admit that they are forms which may be reached by Conversion or other kinds of Immediate Inference to be explained forthwith; but then it has never been deemed necessary or even proper to introduce such among the forms of spontaneous judgment; and if we adopt these we must by parity of reason introduce others, and make the Table contain many more judgments. We are inclined, however, to think that it is of importance to separate those propositions which are Equivalent from others, and to have a letter, U, to designate them. But let it be observed that in the Judgments thus denoted, the notions compared are Percepts or Abstracts. We are thus enabled to retain the old Table, A, E, I, O, for all those judgments in which we have a Concept, while U is added to designate that class of propositions which have been seen to be Convertible since the days of Aristotle, and which turn out to be those in which the notions compared are not general or class notions.

CONJUNCTIONS OF PROPOSITIONS, CONDITIONALS, AND DISJUNCTIVES.

24. We have now to consider propositions in their relations one to another. Most of these relations are of so loose a nature that they cannot be brought under any laws of discursive thought. When we say "the road was long and steep," we have two propositions, "the road was long" and "the road was steep," but with no special connection except that in both the affirmation is made of "road." When we say that "the fever was virulent, but the patient recovered," we have two affirmations so far in a state of opposition, but not involving any discursive process falling under Logic. Such connections of sentences are indicated by connective particles, such as "and," "but," "then," "afterwards," "either," "neither," "so," "however," and attempts have been made by grammarians, with only imperfect success, to classify them into conjunctive, adversative, &c.

25. But propositions may be so connected as to involve a discursive process falling under the laws of thought. We do not refer now to that formal conjunction of propositions which forms reasoning, but to the throwing of two or more connected propositions into one. The propositions hitherto considered are called Categorical, in which one proposition is simply said to agree or not to agree with another. But there are propositions in which the predication is made hypothetically, and which are therefore called Hypothetical. They are of two kinds, one called Conditionals, the other Disjunctives.

26. There are CONDITIONALS OR CONJUNCTIVES in which the predication is made under a condition. "If the night continues clear there will be dew on the grass." Here we have two categorical propositions, "the night is clear" and "dew will be on the grass," and we put them into one proposition, which affirms that they are so related that the one depends on the other. It is certainly desirable in every way to have the propositions spread out and their connection intimated in the conditional form, as it is only thus we can perceive fully the relations of things and of thoughts. But it is of equal importance that we should be able to detect the one proposition in the affirmation that they agree, and that we should be able to point out its subject, its predicate, and copula.

27. The proposition on which the other depends, whether placed first or last, is called the Antecedent, that which depends on it the Consequent, and the relation between them the Consequence. Sometimes there are four terms in the Conditional. "If the sun attracts in the same line as the moon, the tides are at the highest." Here we have four terms; "sun," "attracting in the same line as the moon," "tides," "at the highest." But in propositions with such a connection it will often happen that the same term appears both in the antecedent and consequent, either as subject or as predicate. "If the man pursues an honest course he will prosper." "If virtue is voluntary, vice is voluntary." In all cases the two propositions are put into one in the Conditional, and we have to find the one subject and the one predicate in the affirmation. "The night continuing clear," subject; "will have dew on the grass," predicate. "The sun attracting in the same line as the moon," subject; "will have tides at the highest," predicate. All Conditional Propositions are to be regarded as affirmative. Even when we say that "if the night becomes cloudy there will be no dew," the proposition is not to be regarded as negative, for what we affirm is a relation between the cloudiness of the night and the absence of dew.

28. The logician does not require to consider what is the nature of the dependence of the consequent on the antecedent, whether it is in things or in thought, whether it is or is not the relation of cause and effect, or whether the relation of cause and effect is necessary or contingent. He leaves all these questions to the physical investigator or the metaphysician. To him the relation of the two propositions is given, and he has to consider the discursive thought involved in the relation of the two propositions.

29. Conditional propositions may be Equivalent or they may be Attributive, and we are to determine to which class they belong, in the same way as we do in Categoricals. The examples given above are all of Attributives. But when the terms are singular and abstract, we shall have Equivalent Conditionals, *e. g.*, "If the relation be as 4 to 16, it is the same as that of 1 to 4," or, in Categorical form, "the relation of 4 to 16 is the same as the relation of 1 to 4."

30. Disjunctive Propositions express the relation of two or more judgments which cannot all be true, but one or more of which must. It involves two or more judgments brought into one. It proceeds on the principle of Logical Division (P. I., § 58), implying that we have divided a genus into its co-ordinate species. "Judgment" is the genus, and we find in respect of quality that "every judgment is affirmative or negative." Here we have two members in two propositions, "every judgment affirms," "every judgment denies," and we declare that "every judgment either affirms or denies." These cannot both be true, but one or other must, on the supposition that our division of the species is adequate to the genus. In the same way we may have three members, as "all notions are Percepts, or Abstracts, or Concepts." Or we may have four members, as when we say that in respect both of quantity and quality, every proposition is A, or E, or I, or O; or we may have five members if we add U, and say "all propositions are A, E, I, O, or U."

31. All Disjunctive Propositions are Equivalent or Substitutive. The predicates in the above examples, "either affirms or denies," "Percepts, Abstracts, or Concepts," "A, E, I, and O," are not general notions embracing an indefinite number of individuals, but abstract notions to be taken in their full extent.

IMPLIED JUDGMENTS, OR IMMEDIATE INFERENCES.

32. From any given proposition certain others can be drawn discursively by processes which the logician can analyze and express. These have been called Syllogisms of the Understanding by Kant, to distinguish them from Syllogisms of Reasoning. Some British writers call them Immediate Inferences, as distinguished from Mediate Inferences, or reasoning by means of a middle term. We are inclined to designate them Implied or Transposed Judgments. They all flow from the nature of the Notion as above unfolded, from its interpretation, comprehension, extension and denomination, and from the relation of the notions in the proposition.

33. *CONVERSION.* In this process the terms are transposed so that the subject becomes the predicate, and the predicate the subject. In order to its validity, the truth of the converse must be implied in the truth of the exposita or proposition given. The main rule for securing this is, that no term is to be distributed in the converse which was not distributed in the exposita. It may be effected in two or three ways. (1) Simple Conversion, in which the terms are transposed without any change of quantity. This can be done in propositions in E, in which both terms are distributed, and in I, in which neither is, as E "No man is perfect," converted "No perfect being is man;" I "Some men are generous," converted "Some generous beings are men." (2) Conversion by Limitation or per accidens, by changing the quantity. It being given that "all deception is mean," we cannot say "all mean things are deception," but "mean" being undistributed in the exposita, we give it the sign of particularity or non-distribution in the converse, and say, "Some mean thing (or among mean things) is deception." A can be converted in this way, as may also E. (3) It is disputed whether O can be legitimately converted. "Some students are not industrious." We cannot, therefore, say "some industrious are not students," for you would have students limited in the original proposition and distributed in the converse. Some logicians think that conversion may be accomplished by what is called Contraposition, that is, by attaching the negative to the predicate and reckoning the proposition affirmative, thus making the predicate undistributed. "Some students are not-industrious," converted "some not-industrious are students." This is certainly a legitimate discursive process, but seems to imply Privative Conceptions (see *infra*, § 49).

34. *OPPOSITION.* Light is often thrown on the nature of a proposition by its being put in the various forms of what is called Opposition. In Equivalent propositions there is, properly speaking, only one kind of Opposition, that between an affirmative and negative proposition with the same terms. "Common salt is chloride of sodium," its opposite is "common salt is not chloride of sodium." This Opposition is Contradictory: that is, both propositions cannot be true; and yet one or other must be ; and the truth of the one implies the falsehood of the other, and the falsehood of the one the truth of the other.

35. But when we have Concepts in the proposition, then the forms of Opposition become more varied. They are exhibited in the following diagram.

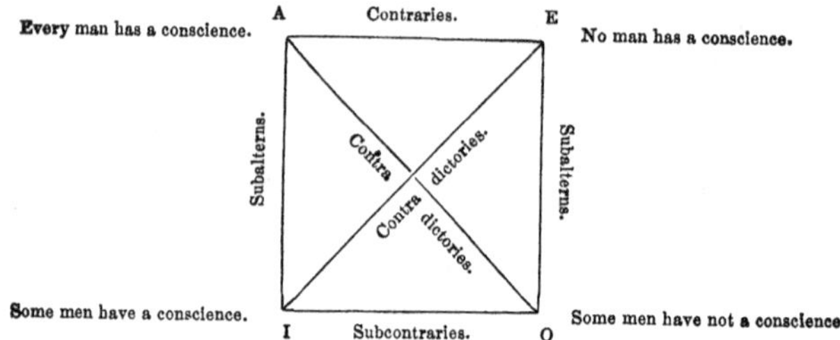

Subalternation, or the relation between two propositions which with the same terms differ in quantity, the one being universal and the other particular. It holds between A and I, between E and O. It can scarcely be said to be a form of Opposition. The rule is, that the truth of the universal implies the truth of the particular. If it be true that "all men have a conscience," it follows that "some men have a conscience." If it be that "no man is free from sin," it is also that "some men are not free from sin." From the falsehood of I we can argue the falsehood of A, and from the falsehood of O the falsehood of E. It is evident that we cannot reversely argue the truth of the universal from the truth of the particular, that we cannot argue A from I or E from O.

36. Subalternation depends on the principle that whatever is true of a class, is true of any and of each of the members of the class. We are now on the very verge of Mediate Reasoning. In Subalternation we say "all bodies attract each other" (A), and so "some bodies attract each other." In Mediate Reasoning we introduce a third term and declare, on the same general principle, that "the planets, being bodies (some bodies), attract each other," (see PART THIRD.)

37. *Contrary Opposition*, in which the propositions, always having the same terms, differ in Quality. It holds between A and E. Contraries cannot both be true. If all men are liars, that is, included in the class liars, it cannot be true that no men are liars. But they may both be false, that is, it may not be true either that "all men are liars," or that "no men are liars." The Opposition between I and O is called Sub-Contrary. They may both be true but cannot both be false. Thus it is true that "some men are liars" and that "some men are not liars." But if it be false, that "some men are sinless," it must be true that "some men are not sinless," and if it be false that "some men have not a conscience," it must be true that "some men have a conscience."

So it is usually said. But it should be observed that in the two last instances we use "some," not in the proper logical sense of 'some at least," "some, we know not how many," but in another sense, "some at most," "some, not all." (See § 7.)

38. *Contradictory Opposition*, in which the propositions differ both in quantity and quality, as A and O, E and I. From the truth of a proposition we can posit the falsehood of its contradictory. If it be true that "all men have a conscience" (A), it cannot be that "some men have not a conscience" (O); and if "some men have not a conscience" (O), it cannot be that all men have a conscience (A). If "no man has a conscience" (E), it cannot be that "some men have a conscience" (I); and if "some men have a conscience" (I), it cannot be that "no man has a conscience" (E). When two propositions are in the relation of contradictories, the truth of the one implies the falsehood of the other, and the falsehood of the one the truth of the other. This is the Law of Contradiction, or, as it is called by Hamilton, of Non-Contradiction. But there is another law involved called the Law of Excluded Middle,—that of two contradictories one or other must be true, there is no Middle between. It must either be that "all men have a conscience" (A), or that "some men have not a conscience" (O); that "no man has a conscience" (E), or that "some men have a conscience" (I). It follows that if you prove the truth of a proposition, you thereby prove the falsehood of its contradictory; or if you prove the falsehood of a proposition, you establish the truth of its contradictory. If you prove that some doctrines, such as the connection of mind and body, are to be believed, though they are not comprehensible, you have thereby shown that a doctrine is not to be disbelieved because it is incomprehensible.

39. Demonstration, that is, the establishment of a point by a pure discursive process founded on truth allowed, is of two kinds, direct and indirect. When the proposition is established by proving its truth, it is said to be direct. We should use this method, as being the most satisfactory, whenever it is available. But there is another mode called indirect which is also valid. You may prove not that a proposition is true, but that its contradictory must be false, which implies the truth of the proposition of which it is the contradictory opposite. Euclid often employs this method of demonstration, showing that you contradict a conceded truth by following any other supposition than that which he makes. We shall see that the same mode is employed in Logic in establishing the Special Rules of the Figures and in certain forms of Reduction.

40. It is desirable in controversy to have the propositions defended, put in the form not of contrary but of contradictory opposition. Without this the combatants may fight without ever facing each other, and the whole discussion will be characterized by hopeless confusion. One asserts that men may be trusted, another that men may not be trusted, and the contest may go on forever with abundant evidence on both sides; but let the positions assume the form "all men are to be trusted" and "some men are not to be trusted," and the question may be settled. One holds that such branches as history and metaphysics should be studied, another that they should not, and both are right and both are wrong; but let the statements be, on the one hand, that "no history is to be studied," or that "no metaphysics are to be studied," and on the other that "some history is to be studied," or that "some metaphysics are to be studied," and the victory will easily be gained by those who hold the affirmative. When arguing with an opponent, let it be your business to prove the contradictory of his position; and you may insist on his proving not the mere sub-contrary of your statement, but the contrary or contradictory. In all cases it is desirable that we should know what is the contradictory (ἔλεγχος) of the proposition we are holding or impugning.

41. The following are the transposed propositions we may obtain by means of Opposition:

If A be true, E is false, I true, O false.
If A be false, E is unknown, I unknown, O true.
If E be true, A is false, I false, O true.
If E be false, A is unknown, I true, O unknown.
If I be true, A is unknown, E false, O unknown.
If I be false, A is false, E true, O true.
If O be true, A is false, E unknown, I unknown.
If O be false, A is true, E false, I true.

From the truth of a universal or falsehood of a particular, we may infer the quality of all the opposed propositions; but from the falsehood of a universal or truth of a particular we can know only the quality of the contradictory.

42. It should be observed that both in Conversion and Opposition we gain the Implied Judgments simply by the contemplation of the Extension together with the involved Comprehension of the Notions. In Subalternation, if A be true, I must be true, because I is involved in the Extension of A. If A be true, E is false, for in A we ascribe an attribute to all A and in E we deny it. In all the transposed judgments we must see that the judgment reached has not a greater Extension than the judgment given, and that we predicate of both the same attribute or group of attributes.

43. Conversion and Opposition are treated of in all the older logical treatises, in which, however, it is not noticed that the propositions reached, are drawn by a contemplation of the Extension and Comprehension of the Notions. Nor has it been explicitly stated that the above rules of Conversion and Opposition do not apply to propositions in which there is no concept. Of such all Conversion is Simple, and all Opposition is Contradictory; thus it being stated that "Newton discovered the law of gravitation," it would be unmeaning to say, by the law of subalternation, that "some Newton discovered the law of gravitation." Later logicians have noticed that there are other Immediate Inferences equally entitled to a place in the exposition of Logical Judgment. It may be doubted whether they have seen their exact nature.

44. *The Interpretation of Judgments* gives certain Implied Propositions. If it be given "the orbit of the planets is elliptical," we have by Denomination "the epithet elliptical may be applied to the orbits of the planets;" by Extension, "the orbits of the planets are among the things that are elliptical," and by Comprehension "elliptical is an attribute of the planetary orbits." Like Transposed Judgments may be derived from propositions in E, I, and O: as O, "some metals are lighter than water," by Denomination the phrase "lighter than water" may be applied to "some metals;" by Extension "some metals may be included in the things which are lighter than water ;" by Comprehension "the property of lighter than water belongs to some metals." Propositions in U may always be interpreted by Denomination and Comprehension. It being given that "Ethics is the science of man's motive and moral nature," we may say "the phrase science of man's motive and moral nature may be applied to Ethics," and "the attributes of the science of man's motive and moral nature belong to Ethics."

45. There are Implied Judgments obtained by the special consideration of the Comprehension of the Notions, as by

The Interpretation of Marks, as when it is said "John loved Jesus," it is implied that "John lived" and that "Jesus lived," and that "there is such a thing as love."

46. *Added Marks* to both subject and predicate. Thus if it be declared that "a negro is a fellow-creature," we may say "a negro in suffering is a fellow-creature in suffering." If "learning be useful" then "injury to learning would be injury to what is useful."

47. *Added Subject and Predicate* may give other judgments by being added to a conception. Thus as "honesty is the best policy," "the disregard of honesty would be the disregard of the best policy."

48. *A Summation of Predicates* may give us an Implied Judgment. Thus if it is found (1) that virtue is voluntary, (2) in obedience to a law, which is (3) the law of God, then we may combine the predicates and get a definition of virtue : "Virtue is a voluntary act done in obedience to the law of God."

49. *Privative Conceptions* may yield Transposed Judgments. We have seen (P. I., § 53) that from any given concept we obtain another by leaving out its mark : thus from the positive concept "wise," we may obtain the privative concept "unwise." Any judgment pronounced on the positive concept, implies judgments upon the privative.

The following is taken from Thomson's *Outlines of the Laws of Thought* (see also De Morgan's *Formal Logic*, p. 61), leaving out the examples in Y :

I. A All the righteous are happy.
None of the righteous are unhappy.
All who are unhappy are unrighteous.

E No human virtues are perfect.
All human virtues are imperfect.
All perfect virtues are not human.

I Some possible cases are probable.
Some possible cases are not improbable.
Some improbable cases are not impossible.

U The just are all the holy.
All unholy men are unjust.
No just men are unholy.

II. A All the insincere are dishonest.
No insincere man is honest.
All honest men are sincere.

E No unjust act is unpunished.
All unjust acts are punished.
All acts not punished are just.

I Some unfair acts are unknown.
Some unfair acts are not known.
Some unknown acts are not fair.

O Some improbable cases are not impossible.
Some improbable cases are possible.
Some possible cases are not probable.

U The unlawful is the only inexpedient.
The lawful is the expedient.
The lawful is not the inexpedient.

We may make a proposition assume any one of these forms as may seem best fitted to give clearness of thought and to enable us to affirm or deny it; and we may express it in the form which may best accomplish the end we have in view in the expression. It is by this process that from O, "some mathematicians have not had much practical wisdom," we get "some without practical wisdom have been mathematicians," (§ 33.) From any one of the above propositions (except those in O) we may derive another proposition by conversion.

50. *Conditional Propositions* give implied judgments. "If this man has consumption he will not recover." This implies that the "case of a man who has a consumption is the case of a man who will not recover," or bringing the notions into closer relation, "One who has consumption will not recover."

51. *Disjunctive Propositions* involve other propositions. Thus if it be allowed that "every given time must be spring, or summer, or autumn, or winter," we are entitled from the rule of Logical Division, that the members must make up the whole (I., § 58), to say, that "all times not spring, or summer, or autumn, must be winter," and from another rule, that the members must exclude one another (I., § 59), to affirm that "winter is neither spring, nor summer, nor autumn."

52. In all these cases the rule is to be rigidly observed, that a term must be distributed in the transposed proposition only when it is distributed in the original one. Because we are entitled to make a predication of some, we are not *therefore* entitled to make the same predication of all.

53. The above are examples of Implied Judgments derived according to rules specified. We believe there may be other kinds drawn by discursive thought, and that the logician could formulize the law which rules them. It may be interesting to show how many other propositions could be got from the single one "men are responsible," by simply contemplating the Extension and Comprehension of the Notions.

EXTENSION.

Every man is in the class responsible.
This man is responsible.

Some men are responsible.
Every tribe of mankind are responsible.
Some responsible beings are men.
It is not true that no men are responsible.
It is not true that some men are not responsible, &c., &c.

COMPREHENSION.

Man exists.
Responsibility is a real attribute.
Responsibility is an attribute of every man.
Responsibility is an attribute of this man.
Responsibility is an attribute of every tribe of men.
Responsibility is an attribute of some men.
Irresponsibility may be denied of all men.
No man is irresponsible.
Irresponsible beings are not men.
Men of wealth are responsible with their wealth.
To punish men is to punish responsible men, &c., &c.

In treating of Implied Judgments we have been indebted to Thomson's *Outlines of the Laws of Thought*, where, however, they are called Immediate Inferences and placed under Reasoning, and are not derived from the nature of the Notions.

54. We may close the part of Logic which treats of Judgment, by showing what Logic can do in settling for us what are and what are not true propositions. It is evident that it cannot determine for us directly what propositions imply and what do not imply Objective reality, *e. g.*, whether there is or is not a sea-serpent. But it can do much in the way of enabling us to pronounce a right judgment upon evidence. It requires us to ascertain what are the Notions, that is, the things compared and in regard to which we make the affirmation or denial. It makes us look at the nature of the notions and find whether they are singulars, abstracts, or general concepts, and to decide about them accordingly. Thus when it is said that "virtue is that which promotes the greatest happiness," we see that both subject and predicate are abstracts, and that therefore the terms must be convertible (§ 14) ; and as we see this, we are better able to determine whether the proposition is true, for we ask whether "that which promotes the greatest happiness is (always) virtue?" If it be maintained that "sea-serpents exist," we perceive that serpent is a common term, and we inquire what are the common qualities (differentia) of serpents, and are thus in a better position to determine whether serpents can exist in the sea, and whether the appearances which sailors have noticed can be of sea-serpents. Logic urges us farther to inquire into the relation of subject and predicate, whether it is one of equivalence or attribution. Every one will admit the truth of the attributive proposition that "virtue promotes happiness," but many deny the truth of the equivalent one, "that which promotes happiness is virtue." We believe that more than one half of the error in the world proceeds not from mere ignorance, but from inattention and confusion, which finding us ignorant, tends to keep us in ignorance. Logic helps to cure the evil by requiring of us to determine what are the notions, and to place these fully and fairly before the mind; and when this is done, we will be able either to see what judgment we should pronounce, or to wait for further light before we come to any decision.

PART THIRD.

REASONING.

1. "In every instance in which we *reason*, in the strict sense of the word, *i. e.*, make use of arguments (I mean *real*, *i. e.*, valid arguments), whether for the sake of refuting an adversary, or of conveying instruction, or of satisfying our own minds on any point, whatever may be the subject we are engaged on, a certain process takes place in the mind which is one and the same in all cases, provided it be rightly conducted. Of course it cannot be supposed that every one is even conscious of this process in his own mind; much less is competent to explain the principles on which it proceeds. This indeed is, and cannot but be, the case with every other process respecting which any system has been formed; the practice not only may exist independently of the theory, but *must* have preceded the theory. There must have been Language before a system of grammar could be devised; and musical compositions previous to the science of Music. This, by the way, will serve to expose the futility of the popular objection against Logic, that men may reason very well who know nothing of it. The parallel instances adduced, show that such an objection might be applied in many other cases where its absurdity would be obvious; and that there is no ground for deciding thence, either that the system has no tendency to improve practice, or that even if it had not, it might not still be a dignified and interesting pursuit."

2. It will be shown that the principles involved in the reasoning process are one and the same, whatever be the things about which we argue, be they material, or mental, or moral, or mathematical, or political, or theological. "One of the chief impediments to the attainment of a just view of the nature and object of Logic, is the not fully understanding, or not sufficiently keeping in mind, the sameness of the reasoning process in all cases. This error may at once be illustrated and removed by considering the parallel instance of Arithmetic, in which every one is aware that the process of a calculation is not affected by the nature of the objects whose numbers are before us ; but that (*e. g.*) the multiplication of a number is the very same operation, whether it be a number of men, of miles, or of pounds." Nor is Logic to be regarded as a peculiar method of reasoning, "which is in fact as great a blunder as if any one were to mistake *grammar* for a peculiar language, and to suppose it possible to speak correctly without speaking grammatically."

3. "Supposing it then to have been perceived that the operation of reasoning is in all cases the same, the analysis of that operation could not fail to strike the mind as an interesting matter of inquiry. And moreover, since (apparent) arguments which are unsound and inconclusive, are so often employed, either from error or design, and since even those who are not misled by these fallacies are so often at a loss to detect and expose them in a manner satisfactory to others, or even to themselves, it could not but appear desirable to lay down some general rules of reasoning applicable to all cases, by which a person might be enabled the more readily and clearly to state the grounds of his own conviction, or of his objection to the arguments of an opponent, instead of arguing at random without any fixed and acknowledged principles to guide his procedure. Such rules would be analogous to those of Arithmetic, which obviate the tediousness and uncertainty of calculations in the head; wherein after much labor, different persons might arrive at different results, without any of them being able distinctly to point out the error of the rest. A system of such rules, it is obvious, must, instead of deserving to be called 'the art of wrangling,' be more justly characterized as 'the art of cutting short wrangling' by bringing the parties to issue at once, if not to agreement, and thus saving a waste of ingenuity."—Whately's *Elements, Analytical Outline.*

4. In Judgment Proper, we compare immediately the two notions, that is, the things apprehended, and declare their agreement. But there are cases in which we do not perceive the relation of the notions immediately, but in which we may discover them mediately, by means of a third or mediating notion. Thus I wish to know whether John the Baptist was a priest, and I cannot pronounce an immediate judgment, for it is not expressly said in Scripture that he was a priest. But we remember that his father Zacharias was a priest, and using son of a priest as a middle term, and finding from the Old Testament that the sons of priests were themselves priests, we argue that "the Baptist, being the son of a priest, was a priest." Here, it will be observed, we have three terms, the two terms we wish to compare, "Baptist" and "priest," and the term by which we compare them, "son of a priest." In the discursive process, when we analyze it, there will be found three acts of comparison: one in which we compare one of the original terms with the middle; a second in which we compare the other original term with the middle; and the third in which we bring the two terms, which we have compared separately with the middle, into comparison with each other. This is Reasoning which is defined as "the act of proceeding from certain judgments to others founded on them."

5. To bring out the acts of comparison involved, we unfold them in three propositions:

> The sons of priests were priests;
> The Baptist was the son of a priest;
> The Baptist was a priest.

When reasoning is thus analyzed and expressed, it is called a Syllogism.

6. The syllogistic analysis of reasoning, so far as is known, was first unfolded by Aristotle in the *Prior Analytics*, and constitutes the most certain, and altogether the greatest, discovery ever made in mental science. It has been discussed, and attempted improvements made on it, by commentators on Aristotle, by the medieval scholastics, by the logicians of the 17th century, and by modern writers from Kant to the present time.

7. Some have thought that we can reason from one judgment. And it is quite true that from any one judgment we can draw others immediately in the mode explained in speaking of Implied Judgments. But the judgments thus reached are confined within very narrow limits. When we have two judgments in a certain relation to each other, a much wider range of judgments can be drawn, and the process involved constitutes Mediate Reasoning, or Reasoning Proper. It often happens, indeed, that in reasoning thus understood, there is only one judgment expressed in what is given or allowed. But if we carefully examine the process it will be found that there is another judgment, which though suppressed in statement, is involved in thought. A man has taken arsenic and we conclude that he shall die. Here are two judgments implied in order to the validity of the reasoning. One is, the matter of fact that he has taken arsenic; and the other, the general fact that he who has drunk arsenic shall die. We may not think it necessary to enunciate both of these. We would not mention the one to a person who had seen him take the arsenic ; we would not announce the other to a man who knew that arsenic was poison. But we would have to state both to one ignorant of both ; and both if not explicitly announced are implicitly implied in the reasoning.

An argument with one premiss suppressed is vulgarly called an Enthymeme. Aristotle, however, defines Enthymeme *ἐνθυμημα μὲν οὺν ἐστὶ συλλογισμὸς ἔξ εἰκότων ἤ σημείων* (Anal. Pr. II., 27. See Hamilton's *Discussions*, Art. *Logic*, and Trendelenburg *Elementa*, § 37).

8. In a syllogism as an analysis of the reasoning process we must have, as we have in the reasoning process itself, three, and no more than three terms : the two whose agreement or disagreement we are seeking to determine, and a third by which we determine it. The two first are called the Extremes, and the third the Middle. Again in a syllogism, in order to unfold the relation of the three terms, there must be three propositions, two in which we compare each of the Extremes with the Middle, and a third in which we compare them with each other. The two first are the Premisses, and the third the Conclusion. It is evident that the Middle term will appear in each of the premisses, but not in the conclusion. The laws of discursive thought do not require us to follow any order in the arrangement of the three propositions. What we have to look at is the relation of the terms ; and if we bring out this, it is no matter whether we begin with the premisses, or which of the premisses we place first. Thus instead of the order followed above, we might say,

The Baptist was a priest ;
for, He was the son of a priest ;
and, The sons of priests were priests.

From these definitions and general statements we may derive certain Rules, which are applicable to reasoning of every kind.

9. (1) In a syllogism there should only be three terms. This has already been explained.

10. (2) In a syllogism there can only be one middle term. It is only thus we can bring the extremes into comparison. When a middle term is ambiguous we may have two middle terms in sense though not in sound; and we are ever liable to compare the one extreme with the middle used in one sense, and the other extreme with the middle in another sense. Hence the fallacy of Ambiguous Middle which will often fall under our notice.

11. (3) One premiss must be affirmative. In other words two negative premisses prove nothing. For unless there be an affirmative judgment declaring the agreement of the middle with one of the extremes, there can be no inference about the terms which we wish to compare. Two negative judgments simply declare that there is no relation between the middle term and the extremes, and authorize no judgment as to the relation of the extremes.

12. (4) If either premiss is negative, the conclusion must be negative. For one of the premisses being negative, the other is affirmative, and so in one premiss we assert that the middle disagrees with one extreme, and in the other that it agrees with the other extreme, and if so the extremes must disagree with one another.

13. (5) To prove a negative conclusion one of the premisses must be negative. We cannot argue that there is no connection between the extremes till we have shown that there is no connection between one of the extremes and the middle.

14. The question now rises, can we determine and enunciate what is the principle in the mind which regulates reasoning. The answer is that this can be done by carefully observing examples of valid reasoning, by ascertaining what is common to them all, and expressing this in a general formula. The rule in its most general form is, that "notions which agree with one and the same notions agree with one another." This for affirmatives, and for negative conclusions "notions which disagree with one and the same notion disagree with one another." But in such a rule the phrases "agree" and "disagree" are wide and vague, and it is desirable to become more particular and specify the nature of the agreement. The distinction which we have drawn between percepts and abstracts on the one hand and concepts on the other (P. I., § 38), leading to the distinction between propositions in which the relation is one of equivalence, and those in which it is one of joint extension and comprehension (P. II., § 14, 15), will help us here, and show us two regulating principles emerging for two kinds of reasoning.

15. *FIRST REGULATING PRINCIPLE.* "Notions equivalent to one and the same third notion are equivalent to one another;" and for negative reasoning "notions which are not equivalent to one and the same notion are not equivalent to one another." This dictum rules all reasonings in which the three notions are Percepts or Abstracts.

Shakespeare wrote Hamlet;
He who wrote Hamlet is the greatest English poet;
∴ Shakespeare was the greatest English poet.

Under this same head I place the following, and indeed most arithmetical and geometrical inferences:

$$A = B$$
$$B = C$$
$$A = C$$

In all ratiocination of this description, the subject of each of the propositions may be made the predicate, and the predicate the subject, and the reasoning will be valid and formally correct.

He who wrote Hamlet was Shakespeare ,
He is the greatest English poet who wrote Hamlet ,
∴ The greatest English poet was Shakespeare.

In these and in like propositions, the terms are percepts or abstracts, and the relations in the propositions and in the argument is of identity or of equality. It is of great moment to separate these simple cases of reasoning from more complex ones, to be immediately considered, in which we have concepts, and extension, and minor and major terms, and mood and figure.

16. We are now in a position to understand what we should make of the unfigured syllogism of Hamilton.

Copperas and sulphate of iron are identical ;
Sulphate of iron and sulphate of copper are not identical ;
∴ Copperas and sulphate of copper are not identical.

Here he has turned " identical," which is neither less nor more than the copula, into a separate term. The reasoning should stand thus :

Copperas is sulphate of iron ;
Sulphate of iron is not sulphate of copper ;
∴ Copperas is not sulphate of copper.

17. *SECOND REGULATING PRINCIPLE.* "Whatever is predicated of a class may be predicated of all the members of that class." In the affirmative form, the *Dictum de omni,* it is, " Whatever is affirmed of a class may be affirmed of all the members of the class." In the negative form, the *Dictum de nullo,* it is, " Whatever is denied of a class may be denied of all the members of the class." It is otherwise expressed, " Whatever is predicated of a concept distributed may be predicated of all that is contained in the concept." This is the famous Dictum of Aristotle, which has been held to be the regulating principle of reasoning by most logicians from the time of the Stagyrite. We hold it to be the true regulating principle in all reasoning in which there is a General Notion. It must be so from the very nature, from the very meaning, of a General Notion, and the employment of it in reasoning. For it will be found that in the reasoning which contains a concept, there is a predication in regard to the concept generally, and a predication in regard to a class or individuals contained in it, and the conclusion is necessitated by the two, or rather by the relation of the two, the one embracing the other in its extension.

18. At this point it will be necessary to explain some terms which are found in attributive (but not in equivalent) reasoning. The subject of the conclusion is called the Minor Term, and the predicate the Major Term: this because the Minor Term (at least in affirmative propositions, P. II., § 17) is the least extensive, and the Major Term the more extensive. The premiss containing the Major Term is called the Major Premiss—sometimes also the Sumption; that containing the Minor Term, the Minor Premiss—or the Subsumption; and this, whichever of the premisses is placed first.

From the time of Aristotle to that of Boethius, the minor premiss was placed first—following the analytic mode; from the time of Boethius it has been customary to put the major premiss first—following the synthetic method.

19. The Dictum of Aristotle is the regulating principle of all reasoning in which there is a Concept. But in order to secure that arguments be put in correct form, logicians lay down certain rules derived from it. These rules are additional to those given above (§ 9–13), as applicable to all reasoning.

20. (1) The middle term must be distributed at least once (by being the subject of a universal or predicate of a negative). For if it were taken only in part, it might happen that in the one premiss we compared an extreme with one part of the middle, and in the other premiss the other extreme with another part of the middle, and thus entirely failed to bring the extremes into comparison.

When this rule is violated, we have the fallacy of Undistributed Middle :

All good men are sincere ;
Rousseau was sincere ;
∴ Rousseau was a good man.

Here the Middle Term is undistributed in both premisses, being the predicate of two affirmatives (P. II., § 11). What we have done is to declare that all good men are among the "sincere," that Rousseau is among the "sincere ;" but then Rousseau may be among the sincere, and not among the good, of whom it is said that they are among the sincere, but not that they are coextensive with the sincere. But it is enough that the middle be once distributed, for as one extreme has been compared to the whole of the middle, even though the other be compared to only a part, we have brought the two into comparison.

21. (2) No term must be distributed in the conclusion which has not been distributed in one of the premisses. Otherwise we should be using a term in its entire extent in the conclusion when we had only made a comparison of it in part of its extent in the premiss. The violation of this rule is called an Illicit Process of the Major or Minor Term, according as it is the major or minor term which is thus illegitimately used.

Whatever gives pleasure is to be valued ;
The learning of logical formulæ does not give pleasure ;
∴ is not to be valued.

Here "to be valued" is taken only in part in the premiss, being the predicate of an affirmative, whereas it is taken in all its extent in the conclusion, and we have an illicit process of the major term.

22. (3) From two particular premisses, no conclusion can be drawn. For if they were both negative (O O), you could get no inference (§ 11). If they were both affirmative (II.), the middle would be undistributed in either premiss (P. II., § 11). There is left only I O, where the conclusion being negative makes the major term distributed, which it is not in the major premiss where it is particular.

23. (4) If one of the premisses be particular, the conclusion must be particular. By a like process to that followed in Rule (3), it can be shown that the violation of this rule implies an illicit process of the minor.

24. It should be observed that these rules apply simply to reasoning in which we have a concept. The rules given from § 9 to § 13, apply to all reasoning. The main rules are summed up by logicians in the following mnemonic lines:

Distribuas medium; nec quartus terminus adsit.
Ultraque nec præmissa negans, nec particularis.
Sectetur partem conclusio deteriorem.
Et non distribuat, nisi cum præmissa, negetve

To understand the third line, that the conclusion follows the *worse* part, it is necessary to bear in mind that logicians reckon the particular as worse than the universal, and the negative worse than the affirmative.

25. *MOODS.* By Mood is meant the legitimate forms of the syllogism indicated by the symbolic vowels A, E, I, O, designating the quantity and quality of the propositions in their respective order.

E No planet twinkles;
A That body twinkles;
∴ E It is not a planet.

As there are four kinds of propositions, and three propositions in each syllogism; and as any one of the four may be the major premiss; and each of the four majors may have four different minors; and each of the sixteen pairs of premisses may have four different conclusions, it might look as if the possible moods might be $4 \times 4\ (= 16) \times 4 = 64$. But many of these moods are illegitimate as violating the rules of the syllogism as above laid down (§ 20–23); some from negative premisses, some from particular premisses, &c. When sifted it will be found that there remain only eleven legitimate moods, AAA, AAI, AEE, AEO, AII, AOO, EAE, EAO, EIO, IAI, OAO.

26. The rest are excluded for the following reasons:

EEA, EEE, EEI, EEO, EOA, EOE, EOI, EOO, OEA, OEE, OEI, OEO, OOA, OOE, OOI, OOO, = 16 for negative premisses.

IIA, IIE, III, IIO, IOA, IOE, IOI, IOO, OIA, OIE, OII, OIO, = 12 for particular premisses.

AEA, AEI, AOA, AOI, EAA, EAI, EIA, EII, IEA, IEI, OAA, OAI, = 12, because of a negative premiss without negative conclusion.

AIA, AIE, AOE, EIE, IAA, IAE, IEE, OAE, = 8, because of a particular premiss without particular conclusion.

AAE, AAO, AIO, IAO, = 4, because of negative conclusion without negative premiss.

IEO is rejected for an illicit process of the major in every figure.

27. FIGURE. This consists in the position of the middle term in reference to the extremes. As the middle term is the very bond of the argument, syllogisms may be divided very conveniently in respect of figure. In the First Figure, the middle term is the subject of the major premiss and predicate of the minor. In the Second Figure it is the predicate of both premisses. In the Third Figure it is the subject of both. In the Fourth Figure it is the predicate of the major premiss, and subject of the minor. Let P stand for the major term (the predicate of the conclusion); S for the minor term (the subject of the conclusion); and M for the middle term.

28. Fig. I. M P A All human beings are responsible to God;
S M A The negro race are human beings;
S P A They are responsible to God.

The Dictum is applicable at once to an argument in this figure. We affirm P (responsible) of M (human beings), and M (human beings) of S (negroes), and in the conclusion we affirm P (responsible) of S (negroes). This figure admits of four moods, AAA, EAE, AII, EIO. From this it appears that it admits of conclusions in every kind of proposition, A, E, I, O; and it is the only figure in which a universal affirmative (A) can be drawn. We shall see when we come to consider Reduction that every kind of argument can be made to take this form; but there are arguments which fall naturally into other figures.

29. There are Special Rules to guide us in determining what are legitimate moods in each figure. Thus for the first figure: (1) The minor premiss must be affirmative; for if it were negative the conclusion must be negative and distribute the major term (P), which would not be distributed in the major premiss, which must be affirmative when the minor is negative. (2) The major premiss must be universal; for if it were particular, the middle term (M) would not be distributed in the major premiss, and could not be distributed in the minor premiss as being the predicate of an affirmative.

30. Fig. II. P M A Reptiles bring forth their young by eggs;
S M E The rat does not bring forth its young by eggs;
S P E The rat is not a reptile.

Arguments fall naturally into this figure when we have to disprove something which has been maintained or believed (as when we prove that the rat is not a reptile), or when we have to bring out the differences of things, which we do by the negative premisses and conclusion.

31. The Special Rules are (1) One of the premisses must be negative, to admit of M being distributed. (2) The conclusion must be negative, because of the negative premiss. (3) The major premiss must be universal, for the conclusion being negative distributes P, which must be distributed in the premiss. The special regulating principle is the *Dictum de Diverso*, "if one term is contained in, and another excluded from, a third term, they are mutually excluded."

32. Fig. III. M P A The connection of soul and body is to be believed;
M S A The connection of soul and body is incomprehensible;
S P I Some things incomprehensible are to be believed.

Arguments fall into this form when the middle term is singular, since a singular term is naturally the subject when the predicate is a concept. It is, therefore, useful in bringing in examples. It is also efficient in establishing an exception to an opponent's premiss, when his argument requires the premiss to be universal. Thus, some one maintains that certain Scripture doctrines are not to be believed, as they are incomprehensible. In order to the validity of his argument it is necessary to assume as his major premiss, that "everything incomprehensible is not to be believed" (E). Now we can, as in the example, show in opposition to him, that "some things incomprehensible are to be believed" (I), which is the contradictory of his major premiss.

33. The Special Rules: (1) The minor premiss must be affirmative. For if it were negative the conclusion would be negative, and would distribute P, which cannot be distributed in the major premiss, which must be affirmative when the minor is negative. (2) The conclusion must be particular, otherwise there would be an illicit process of the minor, which as the predicate of an affirmative is not distributed in the premiss, and cannot therefore be distributed in the conclusion. Its special rule is the *Dictum de exemplo*, "Two terms which contain a common part partially agree, or if one contains a part which the other does not, they partially differ."

34. Fig. IV. P M A What is expedient is conformable to nature;
M S E What is conformable to nature is not hurtful to society;
S P E What is hurtful to society is not expedient.

The Special Rules are (1), Major premiss not O, else illicit major. (2) Minor premiss not O, else middle not distributed. (3) Conclusion not A, else illicit minor.

35. The fourth figure is not found in Aristotle, and many logicians have rejected it. In the minor premiss, S, the predicate is more extensive than M, the subject; and in the major premiss, M, the predicate is more extensive than P; consequently S is more extensive than P. But in the conclusion we find S, the more extensive, the subject, and P, the less extensive, the predicate, which is not agreeable to spontaneous thought, and should not have a place in reflective thought. Figure fourth is perfectly valid, but is not a form into which thought spontaneously falls. It is reached by conversion or other forms of transposed judgments. To take the example (Whately's): the conclusion is not in the form which natural thought would use; we should rather say, "What is expedient is not hurtful to society." This makes "what is expedient" which has been placed as if narrower than "conformable to nature" in the first premiss, which has again been placed as if narrower than "hurtful to society" in the second premiss, to take its proper place in the conclusion as the subject, as narrower than "hurtful to society" in the predicate. But in this collocation the reasoning is in the first figure, which is its natural form.

What is conformable to nature is not hurtful to society;
What is expedient is conformable to nature;
What is expedient is not hurtful to society.

36. *Mnemonic Lines,* devised to exhibit the available moods in each figure, and also to assist in Reduction.

Fig. I. bArbArA, cElArEnt, dArII, fErIOque prioris;
Fig. II. cEsArE, cAmEstrEs, fEstInO, bArOKO, secundæ;
Fig. III. tertia, dArAptI, dIsAmIs, dAtIsI, fElAptOn,
bOkArdO, fErIsOn, habet; quarta insuper addit.
Fig. IV. brAmAntIp, cAmEnEs, dImArIs, fEsApO, frEsIsOn.
Quinque subalterni totidem generalibus orti,
Nomen habent nullum, nec si bene colligis, usum.

In these lines the vowels indicate the mood of the syllogism, *e. g.*, AEE in Camestres (Fig. II.) denotes that the major premiss is universal affirmative, and the minor premiss and conclusion both universal negative. The five subaltern moods which might be drawn, are AAI, EAO, in Fig. I.; EAO, AEO, in Fig. II., and AEO, in Fig. IV.; but they are useless, as universals can be drawn, and they are comprised in AAA, EAE, EAE, AEE, AEE.

37. *REDUCTION.* In this we bring a syllogism in one Figure into the form of a syllogism in another. It is possible to reduce syllogisms in the first figure to syllogisms in the others. But the phrase is specially applied to that process in which we turn syllogisms of the second, third, and fourth figures into the first. The object of reduction is first to show that the Dictum of Aristotle, which is obviously the regulating principle in the first figure, is truly the regulating principle in all reasoning—in which a concept is involved. But it shows secondly, and in a very interesting way, that the reasoning process, whatever be the forms which it takes spontaneously, or those in which it is made to appear by logicians in order to bring out the nature and validity of the process, is in all cases one and the same in substance and in principle.

38. The reduction is made in every instance by Implied Judgments, specially by Conversion; that is, we put one or more of the propositions in a transposed form. The mnemonic lines are meant to direct us in this. The initial consonants b, c, d, f, show that the mood so marked in the second, third, and fourth figures, is to be reduced to the mood marked by the same letter in the first. Thus c in camestres, shows that the syllogism is to be reduced to celarent in the first. The consonants in the middle of the words, show how the reduction is to be effected. Thus *s* indicates that the proposition designated by the vowel before it, is to be converted simply; *p*, that it is to be converted per accidens; and *m*, that the premisses between which it stands are to be transposed. The *k* in baroko and bokardo denotes that the mood is to be reduced *per impossibile*—a process to be explained forthwith.

39. *Ostensive Reduction* is accomplished directly by Conversion and other Implied Judgments. We may give an example from each figure:

Fig. II. cA All men have the power of speech;
mEs Gorillas have not the power of speech;
trEs Gorillas are not men.

reduced to cE Beings having the power of speech are not gorillas;
lA All men have the power of speech;
rEnt Gorillas are not men.

Fig. III. dA Theft is a crime;
tIs Some kinds of theft were encouraged by the laws of Sparta;
I Some of the things encouraged by the laws of Sparta were crime;

reduced to dA Theft is a crime;
rI Some things encouraged by the laws of Sparta were theft;
I Some things encouraged by the laws of Sparta were crime.

Fig. IV. brA Political economy is a profitable study;
mAn Profitable study sharpens the intellect;
tIp Among the things that sharpen the intellect is political economy.

reduced to bAr Profitable study sharpens the intellect;
bA Political economy is a profitable study;
rA Political economy sharpens the intellect.

40. *Reductio per Impossibile.* In this process we proceed on the principle that of two contradictory propositions, one must be true and the other false. We prove not that the original conclusion is true, but that its contradictory must be false. By it the older logicians reduced the syllogisms AOO in the second figure, and OAO in the third. The method of effecting it is indicated by baroko and bokardo in the mnemonic lines, where the letter k intimates that the proposition denoted by the vowel immediately before it must be left out, and the contradictory of the conclusion substituted:

bO Some poets are not wise;
kAr Poets are men of genius;
dO Some men of genius are not wise.

If this conclusion is not true, its contradictory must, "all men of genius are wise." Let this be substituted for the major premiss:

bAr All men of genius are wise;
bA All poets are men of genius;
rA All poets are wise.

This is the contradictory of the originally granted major

premiss, and must therefore be false. But one of the premisses which proves a falsehood must be false. This cannot be the minor, which was one of the originally granted premisses; it must therefore be the major. But this major thus shown to be false, is the contradictory of the original conclusion, which must therefore be true. The same mode of demonstration is employed for baroko, and may be employed in the reduction of all the moods of the second, third, and fourth figures. But it is not necessary to resort to this method. For while baroko and bokardo cannot be reduced by Conversion either simple or per accidens, they may by the Implied Judgments involved in Privative Conceptions, (P. II., 49).

dA All true poets are men of genius;
rI Some not wise are poets;
I Some not wise are men of genius;
or, Some men of genius are not wise.

If we adopt this method, which is perfectly legitimate, quite as much so as that by conversion or contradictory opposition, then we require to substitute fakoro and dokamo in the place of baroko and bokardo in the mnemonic lines.

41. Generally it may be remarked, that in all Mediate Reasoning we may use what are called Immediate Inferences. We may put either of the premisses or the conclusion in the form of any Implied Judgment, if thereby we are enabled to see the relation of subject and predicate more clearly. Thus in the last example the conclusion may be expressed either "some men not-wise are men of genius," or "some men of genius are not wise." This enlarges indefinitely the number of forms in which reasoning may be expressed and still be valid. It is not necessary to spread out all the forms which reasoning may thus be made to take. It is enough to know what we are entitled to do, and how to do it legitimately, when perspicuity of thought requires it.

42. *REASONING IN COMPREHENSION.* In reasoning, so far as we have considered it, the propositions have been understood in extension, and Aristotle's Dictum, which is a maxim in extension, has been considered the regulating principle. But we have seen that all propositions have a meaning in comprehension. May there not then be reasoning in comprehension also? In answering this question fairly, it should be allowed that in the greater number of propositions, the uppermost thought is in comprehension rather than extension. When we are saying "the boy plays," we are thinking of the boy as engaged in the act of playing, rather than among the class of things that play. But it is different when we consider judgments so connected as to entitle us to draw a conclusion. The uppermost spontaneous thought seems now to be in extension. When we argue that "the Red Indian, having the power of speech, is a human being," we refer, in thought, the Red Indian to a class composed of those who have the power of speech. Of course the possession of attributes is implied in each of the terms; but in the ratiocination we require to proceed on the principle that there are classes possessing the attributes; and it is because this is recognized, that the conclusion is seen to follow. If we argue that "man, being responsible, is a free agent," the reasoning is conclusive only on the condition that the whole class "man" is in the class "responsible," which again is in the class "free agent." That "brutes have no free will" cannot give the conclusion that "the brutes are not responsible," unless we proceed on the general principle that "those who are without free will are not responsible."

43. But then all the propositions in a syllogism may be understood in comprehension; and a syllogism may be constructed in which the comprehension is the more prominent, and the reasoning will be perfectly valid, and the form accurate, though not the form expressing the thought which the mind spontaneously follows. The regulating principle will now be, "a part of a part of an attribute will be part of the whole attribute."

Free will is an attribute of responsibility;
Responsibility is an attribute of man;
∴ Free will is an attribute of man.

Bringing forth its young by eggs is an attribute of reptiles;
Bringing forth its young by eggs is not an attribute of rats;
∴ The attributes of reptiles do not belong to rats.

It will be observed that the order of the terms in the propositions, is here the reverse of what it is when we express the thought in extension. In extension we say in the major premiss "man is responsible," "reptiles bring forth their young by eggs." In the form of extension, the subjects are the less extensive and the more comprehensive; and the predicates the more extensive, and the less comprehensive. But in comprehension the subjects are the more comprehensive and the less extensive, and the predicates the less comprehensive and the more extensive.

What do we mean when we say that in reasoning in comprehension the ruling principle is that "part of the part of an attribute is a part of the whole attribute?" We mean, on the principle that the abstract implies the concrete, that whatever things contain a part must also contain a part of that part, *e. g.*, that men, having the attribute of responsibility, have the attribute of free will involved in that responsibility. We seem thus to be thrown back on extension as the uppermost thought in reasoning.

44. But if it be true that the mind reasons primarily in extension, it is not necessary to draw out the forms in comprehension, the more so as the forms in extension embrace all cases of reasoning—except those proceeding on the principle of Equivalence, which we have placed under a separate head (§ 15). But the student should be able, on demand, to translate reasoning in extension, in the way above indicated, into reasoning in comprehension.

45. *THE TWO DICTA ARE COMBINED.* We have seen in our survey, that there is one rule so general, that it may be held as regulating all reasoning that "notions which agree with one and the same notion agree with one another" (§ 14). But this rule is too vague, as not specifying the nature of the agreement; and so we lay down two more specific rules, the one the rule of Equivalence (§ 15), and the other the Dictum of Aristotle (§ 17)—to which we may add the rule of Comprehension—if we allow reasoning in comprehension (§ 42). But there are cases in which the rule of Equivalence and the Dictum are united:

A Locke lived in the seventeenth century;
U Locke is the greatest of English metaphysicians;
A The greatest English metaphysician lived in the seventeenth century.

This is in the Third Figure, and yet we legitimately draw a universal conclusion, and the reason is that the minor term being an abstract is distributed, is distributed in the minor premiss, and may therefore be distributed in the conclusion.

Both Dicta are involved in Mathematical reasoning, as in the demonstration of Euclid, B. I., Prop. I.

(1) The radii of the same circle are equal to one another;
A C and A B are radii of the same circle (B C D);
A C and A B are equal to one another.

(2) The radii of the same circle are equal to one another;
B C and A B are radii of the same circle (A C E);
B C and A B are equal to one another.

(3) A C = A B; B C = A B ∴ A C = B C.

Under this head should be placed what is called a Perfect Induction, in which we argue that what we have found true of each of the members of a class, must be true of the whole class.

A Shem, Ham, and Japhet were in the ark ;
U Shem, Ham, and Japhet were the whole sons of Noah ;
A All the sons of Noah were in the ark.

In both these examples, two of the terms are singulars involving a process of abstraction (but not of generalization) ; the minor premisses are equipollent, with both terms distributed ; and so the minor term is to be regarded as distributed in the conclusion, which is universal. Of the same description :

A Certain sciences are classificatory ;
U These sciences are Mineralogy, Botany, and Geology ,
A Mineralogy, Botany, and Zoology are classificatory.

46. Sir W. Hamilton has an ingenious mode of exhibiting all the possible forms of reasoning both in extension and comprehension. The scheme shows 36 moods in each of the first three figures (the fourth is not allowed), or, in all, 108. Many of these moods would never occur (so it appears to us) in spontaneous thought, and arise from his giving Y, η, and ω, a place among propositions. Still the scheme is worthy of being looked at as exhibiting along with the forms arising in spontaneous thought, those that may be reached by immediate inferences. The Table, with the explanations, is taken from Thomson's *Outlines of the Laws of Thought.* (See p. 142.)

In this Table M denotes the middle term ; and C and Γ the two terms of the conclusion. A colon (:) annexed to a term denotes that it is distributed, and a comma (,) that it is undistributed. Where the middle term has a : on the right side, and a , on the left, we understand that it is distributed when it is coupled in a judgment with the term on the right, and undistributed when coupled with the other. The syllogisms actually represented are all affirmatives, being twelve in each figure ; and the affirmative copula is the line ▬—, the thick end denoting the subject, and the thin the predicate, of extension. Thus C : ▬— , M would signify "All C is (some) M." In reading off the intension, the thin end denotes the subject. But from each affirmative can be formed two negative syllogisms, by making each of the premisses negative in turn. The negation is expressed by drawing a perpendicular stroke through the affirmative copula ; thus ▬┼—. In the negative modes the distribution of

		Fig. I.	Fig. II.	Fig. III.
A	i.	C : —— : M : —— : Γ	C : —— : M : —— : Γ	C : —— : M : —— : Γ
A	ii.	C, —— : M : ——, Γ	C, —— : M : ——, Γ	C, —— : M : ——, Γ
B	iii.	C, —— : M, —— : Γ	C, —— : M, —— : Γ	C, —— : M, —— : Γ
B	iv.	C : ——, M : ——, Γ	C : ——, M : ——, Γ	C : ——, M : ——, Γ
B	v.	C, —— : M, ——, Γ	C, —— : M, ——, Γ	C, —— : M, ——, Γ
B	vi.	C, ——, M : ——, Γ	C, ——, M : ——, Γ	C, ——, M : ——, Γ
B	vii.	C : —— : M : ——, Γ	C : —— : M : ——, Γ	C : —— : M : ——, Γ
B	viii.	C, —— : M : —— : Γ	C, —— : M : —— : Γ	C, —— : M : —— : Γ
B	ix.	C : —— : M, —— : Γ	C : —— : M, —— : Γ	C : —— : M, —— : Γ
B	x.	C : ——, M : —— : Γ	C : ——, M : —— : Γ	C : ——, M : —— : Γ
B	xi.	C : —— : M, ——, Γ	C : —— : M, ——, Γ	C : —— : M, ——, Γ
B	xii.	C, ——, M : —— : Γ	C, ——, M : —— : Γ	C, ——, M : —— : Γ

terms will remain exactly the same as it was in the affirmatives from which they were respectively formed. The line beneath the three terms is the copula of the conclusion; and in the second and third figures, as there may be two conclusions indifferently, a line is also inserted above, to express the second of them. The mark ⏟ under a mode denotes that when the premisses are converted, the syllogism is still in the *same* mode. But a ⋈ between two modes, signifies that when the premisses of either are converted, the syllogism passes into the other. The middle is said to be *balanced* when it is distributed in both premisses alike. The extremes, or terms of the conclusion, are balanced, when both alike are distributed or both undistributed; unbalanced, when one is and the other is not. Two propositions, or two modes, are balanced, when the distribution of terms is the same in both. A. i. and ii. are *balanced.* B. The other modes are *unbalanced.* Of these, iii. and iv. are *unbalanced* in terms only, not in propositions; the rest in both.

47. The author of this treatise has commented elsewhere on Mr. J. S. Mill's theory of the reasoning process. "The 'really fundamental axiom of ratiocination,' as announced by him is, 'Things which co-exist with the same thing, co-exist with one another;' and 'a thing which co-exists with another thing, with which other a third thing does not co-exist, is not co-existent with that third thing.' But the phrase 'co-exist,' if limited to co-existence in respect of time or space, does not include most important cases of reasoning; and if widened beyond this it becomes meaningless. When we argue that the man having committed murder deserves punishment, the premisses and conclusion have reference, not to space or time, but to far different relations. When we infer from A being equal to B, and B to C, that A is equal to C, we are not making affirmations about co-existence. In explanation, he tells us (Vol. I., p. 202, *footnote*, 6th ed.), 'the co-existence meant is that of being jointly attributes of the same subject.' This statement is still vague, and is not adequate, for it does not specify what is 'the same subject,' and it does not bring out that the attribution involves Extension: but it contains partial truth, and it has a meaning, which we can examine.

This new Dictum gives him the following universal formula:

Attribute A is a mark of attribute B;
A given object has the mark A;
∴ The given object has the attribute B.

But what does this first premiss mean when we translate it from abstractions into concrete realities? As there cannot be an attribute existing separately, or apart from objects, it must mean, 'Whatever objects have the attribute A have the attribute B.' And what is this but the major premiss of the old syllogistic formula? The second premiss requires an explanation. "A given object has the mark A:" this object may be one object or a class of objects. In order to give the formula a meaning, we must interpret it, 'Whatever individual or class has the attribute A has the attribute B; a given object or class C has the attribute A; therefore it has the attribute B.' The new Dictum and new Syllogistic formula are just bad versions of the old ones. I call them bad versions, for the phrase "co-exist" does not bring out the precise relation of the terms on which the thought proceeds; and the phrase, "Attribute A," requires to be interpreted in order to have a relevant signification."—*Examination of Mr. J. S. Mill's Philosophy.*

48. Some eminent mathematical logicians are seeking to introduce into Logic, reasoning founded on plurative judgments:

Two-thirds of mankind are heathens;
Two-thirds of mankind live in Asia;
∴ Some who live in Asia are heathens.

Now there is no doubt that this reasoning is valid. But so also:

Lias lies above Red Sandstone;
Red Sandstone lies above Coal;
∴ Lias lies above Coal.

But all logicians allow that in the latter case there is a major premiss implied, that "when one stratum lies above a second, and that above a third, the first must be above the third"; and then the minor premiss becomes, "there is such a stratum (Lias), lying above a second stratum (Red Sandstone), which lies above a third (Coal)"; and then the conclusion follows. It is the same in plurative, and indeed in all arithmetical reasoning, there must be a major premiss got from arithmetic, that is, from a region without and beyond pure discursive thought.

CONDITIONAL REASONING.

49. In this, one or both the premisses are conditional propositions. The common form is that in which the major premiss (so called) is a conditional, and the minor a categorical.

ANTECEDENT.	CONSEQUENT.	
If this man has consumption	he shall die;	major premiss.
He has consumption;		minor premiss.
∴ He shall die.		conclusion.

This is called a Constructive Conditional Syllogism: it proceeds on the rule (*modus ponens*), *Affirm the antecedent and we may affirm the consequent.* In the Destructive form the rule (*modus tollens*) is, *Deny the consequent and we may deny the antecedent.*

If this man has consumption he shall die;
He shall not die;
∴ He has not consumption.

But we are not entitled by denying the antecedent to deny the consequent, or by affirming the consequent to affirm the antecedent; for the consequent may follow from some other antecedent. We cannot, by denying that this man has consumption, deny that he shall die; or by affirming that he shall die, that therefore he has consumption; for he may die of some other disease. Hence arise two fallacies in conditional reasoning: one that of denying the antecedent and therefore denying the consequent; the other that of affirming the consequent and therefore affirming the antecedent.

So far for reasoning in which the major premiss has one or more concepts, and in which the proposition is attributive or the relation one of joint extension and comprehension. But there are cases in which the notions are singular or abstract, and in which the proposition is equivalent, U; and in these we can, from the denial of the antecedent deny the consequent, and from the affirmation of the consequent affirm the antecedent. "If Homer wrote the Iliad he is the greatest poet in antiquity." From this we can infer not only (1) that as he wrote the Iliad he is the greatest poet in antiquity; and (2) that he is not the greatest poet in antiquity if he did not write the Iliad; but farther (3), that if he did not write the Iliad he is not the greatest poet in antiquity; and (4) that as he is the greatest poet in antiquity, he must have written the Iliad.

50. The common forms with a conditional major and categorical minor are:

(1) If A is B, B is C (major).
Equivalent and attributive A is B ∴ B is C. B is not C ∴ A is not B.
Equivalent additional A is not B ∴ B is not C. B is C ∴ A is B.
(2) If A is B, C is D; A is B ∴ C is D. C is not D ∴ A is not B.
(3) If A is not B, C is not D; C is D ∴ A is not B.
(4) If A is not B, C is D; A is not B ∴ C is D. C is not D ∴ A is B.
(5) If A is not B, C is not D; A is not B ∴ C is not D. C is D ∴ A is B.
(6) If A is B, either C is D, or F is G.
A is B ∴ either C is D, or F is G. Neither C is D, nor F is G, ∴ A is not B.
(7) If either A is B, or C is D, either E is F, or G is H.
Either A is B, or C is D ∴ either E is F, or G is H.
Neither E is F, nor G is H ∴ neither A is B, nor C is D.

Other conclusions may be drawn when the terms are equivalent, but it is needless to formulize them.

51. Reasoning, being all the while one and the same, will spontaneously take the conditional or categorical form according to the case to which it is applied. We reason and conclude that "a man guilty of murder should be punished." If we know that a particular man committed the murder, the reasoning would take the categorical form, "This man, having committed murder, should be punished." We may not know, however, whether the man has committed the murder, and we simply assert that "this man, if guilty of murder, should be punished," thus declaring the validity of the consequence. But we come to know that he has committed the murder, and we apply the reasoning, and the form spontaneously assumed will be the categorical.

52. There is a sense in which all reasoning is regarded by logicians as hypothetical, that is, he does not, in looking at the validity of reasoning, examine the truth of the premisses. Assuming them to be true, he inquires solely into the relation between them and the conclusion. But in Hypothetical Reasoning Proper, there is a hypothesis in the very enunciation of the argument. The relation of categorical and hypothetical reasoning is analogous to that between the original and derived propositions in Implied Judgments.

53. All conditional reasoning can be reduced to categorical form. This is accomplished by putting the major premiss in a new shape by immediate inference : as "the case of a man committing murder is a case in which he should be punished," or more simply :

He who is guilty of murder should be punished ;
This man is guilty of murder ;
∴ He should be punished.

When in conditional form, the reasoning is to be tried by the rules of conditionals ; when in categorical form by the rules of the syllogism. It will be found that the fallacy of denying the antecedent and thence denying the consequent, corresponds to illicit process of the major or negative premisses, or the introduction of more than three terms. In conditional form, "If this man has consumption he shall die ; he has not consumption ; therefore he shall not die," becomes categorically, "He who has consumption shall die ; this man has not consumption ; therefore he shall not die" (illicit major). The fallacy of asserting the consequent and thence inferring the antecedent corresponds to the fallacy of undistributed middle or negative premisses. With the same majors, "This man shall die, therefore he has consumption," is in conditional reasoning the fallacy of affirming the consequent, and in categorical of undistributed middle. It is evident from these considerations and examples, that conditional reasoning is the same substantially in the relation of the terms as categorical, and that it is governed in thought by the principles expressed in the Dictum of Equivalence and the Dictum of Aristotle.

DISJUNCTIVE REASONING.

54. In it one premiss is a disjunctive proposition, and the other is categorical. The disjunctive proposition proceeds on the principle that the notion is divided into subordinate species, and is governed by the rules of Logical Division (P. I., § 58, 59) : that the species must make up the genus, and that the species must exclude one another. In it there are two or more judgments which cannot all be true, but one or some of which must. In the categorical premiss (called the minor) we make a predication as to one or other of the species, and in the conclusion, we draw an inference as to the other or others :

Lines are either straight or curved ;
The line A B is not straight ;
∴ It must be curved.

Here we find "line" divided into two exclusive species ; we affirm that it is not in the one species and so infer it must be in the other. There is the same process when the members are three :

The Apostles must either have been deceivers, or deceived, or they spake the truth ;
They were not deceivers nor deceived ;
∴ They spake the truth.

Or with four members:

The season must have been spring, or summer, or autumn, or winter;
It was winter;
∴ It could not have been spring, or summer, or autumn.

A fallacy often creeps into disjunctive reasoning in consequence of the division in the disjunctive premiss not being exhaustive. Thus it is argued "either that all our ideas are had from experience, or that there are innate ideas." Then it is shown that "there are no innate ideas," *i. e.*, that the child is not born with ideas; and the conclusion follows that "all our ideas are from experience." But there is a third supposition, which seems the true one, that "there are innate laws or principles in the mind, ready to be called forth by experience." We have given other examples in treating of Logical Division, (P. I., § 58.) The detection of such fallacies requires us to look beyond Formal Logic, but Logic tells us where they lurk.

55. The following are the principal forms (Fowler's *Logic*):

Either A is B, or C is D (major).
(1) A is B ∴ C is not D. (2) A is not B ∴ C is D.
(3) C is D ∴ A is not B. (4) C is not D ∴ A is B.
Either A is B, or C is not D (major).
(1) A is B ∴ C is D. (2) A is not B ∴ C is not D.
(3) C is not D ∴ A is not B. (4) C is D ∴ A is B.
Either A is B, or C is D, or E is F (major).
(1) A is B ∴ neither C is D, nor E is F. (2) A is not B ∴ either C is D, or E is F.
(3) Neither C is D, nor E is F ∴ A is B. (4) Either C is D, or E is F ∴ A is not B.
(5) Either A is B, or C is D ∴ E is not F, &c., &c.

56. Disjunctive reasoning can be reduced to categorical by changing by immediate inference the disjunctive proposition according to the rule of logical division.

All lines not-straight are crooked ,
A B is not-straight ;
∴ It is crooked.

This shows that ultimately disjunctive reasoning is founded on the same principle as categorical, that is, on the principle of subalternation of the species to the genus, implied both in logical division and in the Dictum of Aristotle.

DILEMMA.

57. There are spontaneous exercises of thought in which we draw a conclusion from disjunctive premisses, or reach a disjunctive conclusion without determining which of the alternatives is to be preferred ; and in these the reasoning takes the form of a dilemma. In it we have a conditional premiss, in which either the antecedent or consequent is disjunctive, and in the other premiss we make a predication in regard to the exclusive nature of the disjunctive in the premiss, and thence draw a conclusion.

Major. If a man can help a thing he should not fret about it : if he cannot help a thing he should not fret about it.
Minor. But he can either help a thing or not help it ;
∴ He should not fret about it.

He who opposes this must set himself against one or other of the alternatives—must, as it is said, choose his horn, and if the alternative is exhaustive, he will be transfixed by either. If a dilemma is accurate in form, the conclusion follows, and the only way of meeting it is by showing that the alternatives in the premisses are not exhaustive—that there may be another supposition.

If that narrative be true you must believe it ; if it be false you must disbelieve it ;
But it must either be true or false ;
You must either believe it, or not believe it.

But there may be a third supposition, that it is partly true and partly false. The rules are (1), The antecedent being affirmed, either disjunctively or not, as the case may be, the consequent must be admitted; (2) The consequent being denied, either disjunctively or not, the antecedent must be denied.

58. (1) There are cases in which the first premiss consists of one antecedent and several consequents. The conclusion is destructive.

> If A is B, C is D, and E is F;
> But either C is not D, or E is not F;
> ∴ A is not B.

(2) In which the major consists of several antecedents and one consequent; and we draw the common consequent in the conclusion. The argument is constructive:

> If A is B, or if C is D, E is F;
> But either A is B, or C is D;
> ∴ E is F.

(3) In which each of the antecedents has a different consequent, and we can draw the consequent only disjunctively. The argument may be constructive or destructive:

> Major. If A is B, C is D, and if E is F, G is H;
> Minor. But either A is B, or E is F;
> ∴ Either C is D, or G is H.
> Minor. But either C is not D, or G is not H;
> ∴ Either A is not B, or E is not F.

59. There may be Trilemma or a Tetralemma, &c., when the number of antecedents or consequents, one or both, is three, four, &c. *Trilemma.* If the universe is not the best possible, we must suppose that God did not know a better, or that he could not make a better, or that he did not desire a better. The first supposition cannot be true (for it is inconsistent with His wisdom); and the second (because it limits His power); and the third (because against His goodness); therefore the universe must be the best possible.

60. A Dilemma being a conditional with a disjunctive proposition, may be reduced to categorical syllogistic form, like conditionals and disjunctives.

CHAINS OF REASONING.—THE SORITES.

61. *Prosyllogism and Episyllogism.* Hitherto we have been considering single arguments. But ratiocination is commonly conducted in a train, and the single argument has a connection with what goes before and with what follows. The major or minor premiss, one or both, of any syllogism, may have been established by a previous act of reasoning, which in relation to that syllogism is called a Prosyllogism. Or a syllogism may be employed to establish a position to be used as a premiss in a subsequent syllogism called an Episyllogism. The conclusion in the Prosyllogism is a premiss to the syllogism which it precedes ; the Episyllogism uses the conclusion of the syllogism which goes before as a premiss. It is evident that the same syllogism may be a Pro-syllogism in one connection, and an Epi-syllogism in another.

Pro-Syllogism.	He who administers arsenic administers poison;
	The prisoner administered arsenic ;
	∴ The prisoner administered poison.
Given Syllogism.	He who administers poison is guilty of murder;
	The prisoner administered poison ;
	∴ He is guilty of murder.
Epi-Syllogism.	He who is guilty of murder should be executed;
	The prisoner is guilty of murder;
	∴ He should be executed.

This may become a Prosyllogism to a farther act of reasoning :

He who is to be executed should not be executed in public;
This man is to be executed ;
∴ He should not be executed in public.

This may be taken as an example of a chain of reasoning. It is not to be understood that in spontaneous thought, the mind constructs the reasoning into syllogisms. It is enough that it perceives the relations involved in the terms. The formal unfolding of the relations is left to the logician.

62. Logicians have drawn the form of one of these chained trains of reasoning, and call it the Sorites (from σωρὸς, a heap— the Germans call it chain argument, Kettenschluss) :—The prisoner administered arsenic to the man who died ; he who administers arsenic administers poison ; he who administers poison is guilty of murder ; he who is guilty of murder should be executed ; he who is executed should not be executed in public ; ∴ the prisoner should not be executed in public. The Sorites consists of a series of propositions, the predicate of each becoming the subject of the one following, till in the last step the predicate of the last is affirmed or denied of the subject of the first, which is the conclusion. In the process there are as many middle terms as there are propositions between the first and the last ; and the mind in reasoning sees the connection between these middles and the other terms, and thus passes on from the first premiss to the final conclusion. The Dictum of Aristotle slightly modified, is the regulating principle. "Whatever is affirmed or denied of a whole class, may be affirmed or denied of whatever is comprehended *in any class that is wholly comprehended* in that class,"—the words in Italics being an addition. In the Sorites the first proposition, and that alone (with the last), can be particular ; because in the first figure the minor may be particular but not the major (§ 29), and all the other propositions on to the conclusion are major premisses. There can be one and only one negative premiss, and that the last ; for if any others were negative, one of the syllogisms would have a negative premiss, which cannot be in the first figure.

63. The reasoning is perfectly valid, but we may in the way of testing it, and to show that this form of reasoning is founded on the same principle as the syllogism, draw out the process in a series of syllogisms. These will all be in the first figure; the same in number as the middle terms; and the first will have for its major premiss the second proposition of the Sorites, and for its minor the first. Syllogisms thus drawn out, will take the form of syllogism, pro-syllogism, and epi-syllogism, given above:

The form is, All (or some) A is B;
All B is C;
All C is D;
All (or no) D is E;
∴ All (or some) A is (or is not) E.

Reduced to syllogisms:

All B is C;	All C is D;	All (or no) D is E;
All (or some) A is B;	All (or some) A is C;	All (or some) A is D;
∴ All (or some) A is C.	∴ All (or some) A is D.	∴ All (or some) A is (or is not) E.

The Sorites may take another form called Goclenian (from Goclenius who noticed it). The subject of each premiss becomes the predicate of the next; the conclusion predicates the first predicate of the last subject; the first premiss only can be negative and the last particular. When expanded into syllogisms the conclusion of each becomes the major premiss of the next. The form is:

All (or no) E is F;
All D is E;
All C is D;
All B is C;
All (or some) A is B;
∴ All (or some) A is (or is not) F.

He who is executed should not be executed in public; he who is guilty of murder should be executed; he who administers poison is guilty of murder; and he who administers arsenic administers poison; the prisoner administered arsenic; therefore the prisoner should be executed, but not in public. These two forms differ from each other only as a syllogism with the major premiss put first, and the minor premiss second, differs from a syllogism with the minor premiss put first and the major last (see § 18). A series of Conditional arguments may in the same way be abridged into a Sorites. If A is B C is D; if C is D, E is F. But A is B ∴ E is F.

GENERAL REMARKS ON THE REASONING PROCESS.

64. We have seen that in all reasoning there is involved a comparison of two terms by means of a third, and that when the process is fully unfolded, there will be three propositions, that is, two premisses and a conclusion. The question arises, whence do we get the premisses? The answer is, that they may be obtained either by intuition or by experience. First there are premisses gained by an immediate intuition of objects. It is thus that I know that these two parallel lines will not meet however prolonged; that these two straight lines cannot enclose a space; that this deed of ingratitude to God and cruelty to man is a sin. We reach these truths by no process of inference; we perceive them to be true on the bare contemplation of the objects. But a far greater number of premisses are attained by ordinary observation—in the case of general truths by a gathered observation. It is thus we know that fire burns, that all bodies attract other bodies, that plants and animals need nourishment, and that animals feed on other organized matter.

65. This gathered observation may be made by the individual for himself, or by the combined experience of others. Of these, the individual experience, so far as it goes, is by far the more valuable; as with the results we have the processes which guide and restrain in the application of the general maxim. It is for this reason that a mere school or book learning can never serve the ends of a practical education; and that a dear-bought personal experience is often worth all the labor and suffering which may have been expended in gaining it. But on the other hand, individual observation, however enlarged, must always be limited, and unless widened by intercourse with mankind and by reading, tends to become narrow and exclusive. By far the greater part of any man's knowledge is derived from the experience of others, and is conveyed to him by oral instruction and books; and the most valuable part consists in nice distinctions and scientific laws, some of which embody the results of the thoughts of the greatest men who have appeared on our earth, and of a hundred generations.

66. Some of these have been written out and proclaimed to the world; such, for instance, are ascertained natural laws, as the three laws of motion, the classifications of natural history, the chemical affinities of bodies, and certain laws of the mind, such as those of the logical processes, of intuition, and the association of ideas. It is one of the advantages which the modern reasoner has over the ancient, that he has provided for him and placed at his disposal, an immense number and variety of general principles handed down from the ages precedent. Others of the published maxims are of a moral and practical nature, such as proverbs and wise saws handed down from father to son and from one generation to another, as "Evil communications corrupt good manners," "Second thoughts are best." Others of the maxims have not been embodied in words and never will be. For example, you have discovered of a certain man that you can trust him, and you confide in his statements, and could place your property in his hands. Or, you have found of a certain look and manner, which you know but could not describe, that they are signs of deceit and dishonesty. Such *media axiomata*, as Bacon calls them, equally removed from high generalizations and minute particulars, are most useful of all in the arts and the practical business of life. And observe wherein lies their utility. They form, as we shall immediately see, the major premisses in that reasoning which the mind is ever conducting in regard to the cases that cast up—these cases supplying the minors. One grand use of education in the higher sense of the term, of travel, and of an acquaintance with the world, is to supply such majors for continual use and application in the varied circumstances of life.

67. Many of the maxims are absolutely certain. Such are established scientific laws, as those of chemical affinity, of physiology, and psychology. Such are also all moral maxims, as that it is wrong to lie, to thieve, to kill. In other cases, the maxim is true only in most cases. For example, the rule that netted-leaved plants are exogenous is true only as to most plants; for there is a tribe called dictyogens by Lindley, which have netted-leaves and yet are endogenous. The general observation that solanaceæ are poisonous, has a still greater number of exceptions—for the potato is a solanaceous plant; and all that such a rule can do is to guard against eating the flowers or berries of this tribe of plants when they come in our way. Of this character are the loose maxims which float in the world as to races and nations. Acting on them we are commonly right, while we should greatly err if we insisted on applying them rigidly. "One of themselves, even a prophet of their own, said, the Cretans are always liars, evil beasts, slow bellies," "Frenchmen are lively," "The Irish are witty," "The Scotch are cautious."

68. When all the new steps in the reasoning process are seen to be true intuitively, we have what is called Demonstration (ἀπόδειξις). The fittest example is to be found in Mathematics. Here we start with things defined, that is, with points, lines, squares, ellipses, &c., and looking to these things, on the bare contemplation of them, we discover certain truths regarding them. This is what is to be understood by intuitive truths—truths seen on the bare inspection of the things. Having thus obtained certain truths, we compare two truths by means of a third—which is reasoning—and rise to farther and farther truths. Finding that the line A B = the line C D, and C D = E F, we conclude that A B = E F. The things we thus compare are all abstracts, and the notions are all distributed both in the subject and the predicate. This kind of reasoning all falls under the head in which the law of Equivalence is the regulating principle. We may arrange the terms as we please as subject and predicate in the proposition, and the propositions as we please in the syllogism—there being, properly speaking, no major and no minor. We do not require to announce a general principle, as that things which are equal to the same things are equal to one another; on the bare contemplation of A B and E F being equal to C D, we conclude them to be equal to one another. This reasoning is also found to a limited extent in Formal Logic, as when we draw the rules of the syllogism (§ 20–23) and the special rules of the figures (§ 29–34) from the Dictum of Aristotle. It cannot, however, be employed in any of those departments of knowledge in which we deal with scattered facts. In such branches, the only available method is that of Induction—a subject which does not fall under Formal Logic, but that Secondary department which treats of discursive thought as applied to certain classes of objects.

69. When the evidence is gained from a gathered experience, it is called Experiential, also Probable, and Moral. It is of importance that we should know the difference between this and Demonstrative or Apodictive evidence. (1) The essential distinction is that the one is derived exclusively from intuition, and the other partly or wholly from experience. In order to discover the truth, the mind in the former case looks simply at the object; whereas in the latter there is need of observation, commonly of observation upon observation. There is no need of trial in order to convince us that two parallel lines will never meet; the truth is discovered at once by the bare contemplation of parallel lines. But we cannot by thus inspecting the things say whether the planets do or do not move in ellipses, whether the earth is or is not hot in the centre. "A clever man shut up alone and allowed an unlimited time, might reason out for himself all the truths of mathematics, by proceeding from those simple notions of space and number of which he cannot divest himself without ceasing to think; but he could never tell by any effort of reasoning what would become of a lump of sugar in water, or what impression would be produced on his eye by mixing the colors yellow and blue." (Sir J. Herschel.) (2) The one does not, the other does, admit of degrees. Demonstration does not allow of degrees. Every one proposition so substantiated, is as certain as any other, as every other. Nor can we add to the evidence of a proposition demonstrated. That the opposite angles formed by the crossing of two straight lines are equal, this cannot be rendered more certain by any addition of proof. It is different with observational evidence which admits of all degrees of certainty. That it will rain to-morrow is a vastly more uncertain proposition than that the sun will rise to-morrow. This kind of evidence may have additions made to it; the probability of there being rain may be increased by the fall of the barometer and the threatening aspect of the sky. It may rise at last to moral certainty, which ought to carry our full conviction and lead to corresponding action. (3) In the one there is not, in the other there commonly is, a balancing of seemingly opposite proofs. In Demonstration there never is anything contrary, even in appearance, to what has been established. But in Probable evidence there is often one fact or argument which seems to incline one way, and another which seems to tend the other way; and in order to arrive at a satisfactory conclusion, we must look at both, and give to each its proper weight. What a number of considerations require to be estimated before a merchant makes an extensive purchase of certain goods; before a statesman proposes a measure with far-reaching consequences; before a general ventures on a perilous campaign! The most useful of all kinds of practical sagacity is that which enables a man, in the midst of complicated circumstances, to determine on which side the balance of probability lies. (4) The one does not, the other does, involve responsibility. There is no sort of accountability attaching to intuitive evidence; a man must believe it, whether he will or not. We have no credit, or the reverse, in believing that if we take equals from unequals that the remainders are unequals; or that the angles at the basis of an isosceles triangle are equal to one another. As soon as any one understands these propositions and the evidence advanced in their behalf—if they need proof—he is obliged to yield his assent to them. It is different with Experiential Evidence. A man may or may not listen to it; he may, but he also may not, act upon it. There is room here for the influence of a spirit of candor, or for the opposite temper of prepossession and prejudice. It is on this account, that experiential evidence is often called Moral, because it is possible for us either to attend to it or not to attend to it, and the act to be morally right or morally wrong.

70. It is vain to expect Demonstration in every line of inquiry. Demonstration is confined to a limited class of objects, and these characterized by their simple and abstract nature. In most of the sciences it is not available; it cannot be had in chemistry, in natural history, in psychology, in political economy. In the practical affairs of life no man looks for it. If a man's house is on fire, he will proceed to pour water upon it, though it cannot be demonstrated in the technical sense of the term, that water will quench the flame. The evidence adduced in behalf of the existence of God, of the immortality of the soul, of a day of judgment, and of the truth of the Christian religion, is all of this moral character. It is addressed to an understanding capable of weighing it, and a heart supposed to be ready to receive it. There may be excellence implied in the faith that receives it; and guilt involved in the perverseness which rejects it.*

71. To return from this seeming digression. It is to be observed that all reasoning proceeding on experiential evidence falls under the Dictum of Aristotle, and in order to its validity we must have a major as well as a minor premiss. The major may not always be expressed; the argument often takes the form that is vulgarly called an Enthymeme, that is, with one premiss suppressed. But one reason for its being so often unnoticed is that we are so familiar with it; and whether expressed or not, it is in all cases implied, and we proceed upon it in our reasonings.

72. It has been disputed whether there is reasoning involved in the Inductive Method of inquiry, by which all discoveries have been made in physical and mental science. In that method two steps are involved: one is the gathering of the facts; the other the gathering of the law out of the facts. In the former there may be no special exercise of ratiocination; but in the latter there is; we proceed from something given to something derived from it, from the facts to the law of the facts. And

* "I receive mathematics as the most sublime and useful science as long as they are applied in their proper place; but I cannot commend the misuse of them in matters which do not belong to their sphere; and in which, noble science as they are, they seem to be mere nonsense; as if, forsooth, things only exist when they can be mathematically demonstrated. It would be foolish for a man not to believe in his mistress's love because she could not prove it to him mathematically. She can mathematically prove her dowry, but not her love."—GOETHE'S *Conversations with Eckermann.*

this reasoning can be reduced to syllogistic form. In the inference there are two things involved; one is the facts gathered, and the other some general principle on which we proceed in reaching the law from the facts. Attempts have been made to enunciate the principles which entitle us to rise from the particulars to the laws and causes. The first systematic attempt was made by Bacon, who enumerated a number of Prerogatives of Instances (Prerogativæ Instantiarum), which enable us to proceed from the facts to what he called axioms, causes, and forms. In this past age these have taken a better form in what are called Canons of Induction. Now these Prerogatives of Instances, or Canons of Induction, are in fact the major premisses, while the observed facts constitute the minor premisses in the process by which we rise from the facts to the law. To give an example. The ancients referred the rising of water in a pump, and of mercury in a tube, to nature's horror of a vacuum. Toricelli and Pascal referred it to the weight of the atmosphere. The case was decided by taking a barometer to the top of a mountain, when it was found that the mercury descended as the instrument was carried up to a higher elevation. One of Bacon's Prerogatives of Instances guarantees the process, what he calls the *Experimentum Crucis:* When there are two rival theories, let us produce a phenomenon which can be explained by the one and not by the other, and it will prove the truth of the theory which furnishes the explanation. This constitutes the major premiss, and the minor premiss is the fact that the mercury sinks as the atmosphere becomes lighter,—a fact which cannot be explained on the theory of nature's horror of a vacuum, but can on the other. The process may be unfolded still more clearly by that Canon of Induction called the Method of Difference. "If in comparing one case in which the effect takes place, and another in which it does not take place, we find the latter to have every antecedent in common with the former except one, that one circumstance is the cause of the former, or at least, part of the cause of it." This is the major premiss in the argument. The minor is, that at the foot of the mountain where the atmosphere was heavy the mercury was high, while it was low at the top where the atmosphere was light. The two together guarantee the conclusion that the weight of the atmosphere is the cause, or part of the cause, of the rise of the mercury.

73. The best exposition of the Canons of Induction is by Mr. Mill (*Logic*, B. III., c. viii.). He states and illustrates five :—that of the Method of Agreement, of the Method of Difference, of the Joint Method of Agreement and Difference, of the Method of Residues, and of Concomitant Variations. But he does not perceive that their Canons are the major premiss, while the facts are the minor premiss, in the process by which we reason from the facts to the law. We are prevented from enlarging on this subject only by the circumstance that it would carry us into Particular Logic. It is enough to show here how the reasoning involved in Induction can be reduced to syllogistic form.

74. When the premisses are only probably true, the conclusion is also only probably true. "Rash actions lead to evil consequences," is true only in a general way—there are cases in which rash deeds have led to brilliant results. But in dealing with such general maxims, we are not to allow to the conclusion a certainty not found in the premisses—to use a graphic illustration of Whately's—"The chain is not stronger than its weakest part." It is evident that if both the premisses in an argument, and still more if all the premisses in a chain of argument, be only probably true, the conclusion is more uncertain than any one of them. If a story has reached us through a number of persons detailing it the one to the other, it may come in the end to be very doubtful, even though each narrator be probably trustworthy. It is thus that events, handed down from age to age by tradition, become in the end very uncertain—the stream may at first have been pure, but it receives a polluting mixture in every region through which it passes. Sometimes we can, in a loose way, numerically estimate the probability attaching to each premiss in the chain of proof, and then we can state the conclusion numerically. The incident, we may suppose, has reached us through three persons : one trustworthy, and we value his testimony at $\frac{9}{10}$, regarding 1 as absolute certainty ; the testimony of another we reckon $\frac{3}{4}$, and of the other $\frac{1}{2}$; the probability of the story being true is now $\frac{9}{10} \times \frac{3}{4} \times \frac{1}{2} = \frac{27}{80}$; and we see that the story is more likely to be false than true. The success of a scheme depends, we may suppose, on the combined character and ability and wisdom of the person who manages it. His character we estimate $\frac{9}{10}$; his ability, $\frac{7}{10}$; and his wisdom, $\frac{6}{10}$; the probability of his success will be $\frac{9}{10} \times \frac{7}{10} \times \frac{6}{10} = \frac{378}{1000}$, or the scheme is more likely to fail than to succeed. It is seldom that in the practical affairs of life we can get numerical estimates of any value. When, however, the data are derived from such occurrences as the average number of deaths taking place annually among a definite number of persons, and of fires occurring in a certain description of property, Insurance Companies can make calculations which are rigidly correct as to averages. But in all such cases the calculation belongs rather to the arithmetician than the logician. The shrewd man of the world, without expressing his premisses or conclusion in numbers, can commonly obtain sufficient data to enable him to reason and reach a sound conclusion, as to the side on which the probability lies, in departments falling under his habitual notice. He may err in regard to a given proposal made to him, and lose much by acting or not acting ; but in the long run he will be found in acting on the rules (majors) which he has laid down for himself, to have acted judiciously. He who proceeds habitually on such principles as that "rash actions are to be avoided," "honesty is the best policy," will be found in the end to have acted a prudent part in this world. Swayed by other and moral principles, he will be found to have acted a good and a generous part.

75. When there is a concurrence of evidence towards a particular point, the conclusion is more probable than any of the premisses. An incident is detailed to us by three independent witnesses known to us to be trustworthy, and we have now quite as certain proof as is to be had in this world. We estimate the probability of each of them speaking the truth as $\frac{9}{10}$; this makes the probability of each of them speaking falsely as only $\frac{1}{10}$, and the probability of the three concurring in a falsehood as $\frac{1}{10} \times \frac{1}{10} \times \frac{1}{10}$, or only $\frac{1}{1000}$. Of this description is the evidence in behalf of the great doctrines of natural and revealed religion. Thus in behalf of the existence of God, we have the argument from the evident design in the structure and adaptations of animal and plant, the native disposition to trace the seen effects to their unseen cause, and the conscience or law in the heart pointing to a lawgiver. In favor of the Christian religion we have the deposition of witnesses that Jesus performed miracles and rose from the dead; and we have the character of Jesus and the doctrines he taught, the spirit he inculcated and the precepts he enjoined. Evidence of this kind is called Cumulative, and may amount, as in the cases just mentioned, to the highest moral certainty. There is still, to be sure, a bare possibility of error, but it is as one to a thousand, a million, or a million millions. Only diseased minds will allow themselves to dwell on it—only the fool will say in his heart, There is no God. But healthy minds will brush it aside, will in fact not feel it in the view of the overwhelming evidence on the other side.

76. When there is a concurrence of facts towards a

conclusion, the point may be regarded as established when no one of the proofs is itself sufficient. This is what is called Circumstantial Evidence. A murder has been committed, a person is charged with the crime, and the proof runs as follows :

The murderer may very likely have blood on his clothes ;
This man had blood upon his clothes ;
∴ He is the murderer.
The murderer must have been prowling about the premises ;
This man was prowling about the premises ;
∴ He is the murderer.
The murderer will have some of the goods of the murdered man ;
This man had some of the goods of the murdered man ;
∴ He is the murderer.

No one of these arguments is in itself conclusive. The syllogisms are all in the second figure ; the premisses are both affirmative ; in neither is the middle term distributed, and so no conclusion can be drawn. But by such considerations we reach a general major premiss, that the person thus found with blood on his clothes, thus seen prowling about the premises, and caught with the property of the murdered man in his possession, must be the murderer, and the conclusion follows syllogistically.

77. Whence the rapidity and the unreflective nature of the process ? It is acknowledged by all logicians, that in spontaneous reasoning we have not before us consciously the distinction between major, minor, and middle, the moods and the figures of the syllogism. I hold, indeed, that in all reasoning, the mind has before it the terms, and perceives the relations between them ; but having this, it proceeds with amazing quickness and without analyzing or even reflecting on the process. This rapidity proceeds from the laws of the association of ideas. These laws are those of Coexistence and Correlation. Things which have been together in the mind tend to suggest each other, as do also things that are related, say by resemblance, or means and end, or by cause and effect. Now in subjects with which we are familiar, we have laid up an immense store of such associations, partly by the things having been brought together in our experience, and partly by our being ever called on to notice relations. What a number of such associations are formed in the mind of the mathematician, the mechanic, the politician, and the student of the fine arts, each in his own department. And when he is meditating on any one topic, his thoughts flow on with amazing speed from one point to another. In this flow the terms of an argument or a train of reasoning come up, and he perceives the relations between them, and goes on from premiss to conclusion, and from one conclusion to a farther. Meanwhile he might be quite incapable of unfolding the process, or even of recalling the steps. At the same time it is ever to be understood that the train of ideas raised by association does not amount to reasoning. I believe that much of what is called reasoning in brutes, and even among children, proceeds from mere association. When the burnt child, and we may add the burnt dog, dreads the fire, it is from the mere law of coexistence. All their lives men are, more or less, under the influence of mere association, in cases in which we imagine them to be reasoning. They are led, not by a concatenated train of argument, but by mere impulse—as it is said, that is, by the suggestion that comes up. Hence the mistakes into which they are ever falling—mistakes not to be referred to the reasoning power. In all judgment, and in reasoning as implying judgment, there is a perception of the relations of the notions to each other ; and it is only thus we can reach a sound and safe conclusion. Association is to be allowed to aid us as an assistant, and to suggest terms for comparison. But above it, as a master, there is to be an understanding to judge of the relations of the terms thus brought before the mind ; not that we should adopt them or follow them, but that we should judge of them, and believe and act accordingly.

78. In what sense are the truths reached by the reasoning process new truths, and in what sense old truths? They are old truths, inasmuch as they all depend upon, and are derived from, the truths with which the mind has started in the reasoning process. That this man will die, may depend on two other truths, that he has consumption, and that consumption produces death. That man will have to appear before the Judgment-seat, may depend on other truths, as that he is a moral being, possessing intelligence, conscience, and free will. The truths of the sixth book of Euclid are all obtained from the definitions, axioms, postulates assumed at the beginning, and from the reasonings of the first five books. But in another and an important sense they are new truths. They are not truths at all to us, till they are reasoned out ; they may not be known to us till they have been unfolded by the reasoning process. There are truths, especially in morals, but also in the fine arts, in geometry itself, and indeed in every department of knowledge, thus bursting upon us with all the freshness of novelty, because in fact they are now brought out by us for the first time, from premisses—it may be known to us for years. Such truths, it is often said, come to us by intuition ; but in fact they are obtained by a rapid reasoning process aided by association ; and we forget the steps we have taken in climbing, in the joy we experience because we have gained the height.

FALLACIES.

79. A fallacy is defined "any unsound mode of arguing, which appears to demand our conviction and to be decisive of the question in hand, when in fairness it is not." Its genus is "any unsound mode of arguing;" but every unsound mode of arguing is not a fallacy; it is so only when "it seems to demand our conviction and to be decisive of the question in hand when"—we prefer saying —"it is not according to the laws of thought." In order to its being a fallacy, it is not needful that it should be studiously constructed for deceitful purposes. The man who uses it may himself be deceived by it; or more frequently he has first been deceived by the influence of selfishness or passion, and "the wish becomes father of the thought," and the argument occurs to him and he advances it in his justification. Some logicians call a fallacy a Paralogism, when the man who employs it is deceived by it, and a Sophism when, being aware of its unsoundness, he uses it to deceive others. We need to be warned not only against the sophistry of designing men, but against the fallacies laid in our way by persons who believe what they say; and, as still more dangerous, against those which originate in thoughts that favor our own selfish and crooked aims.

80. In order to avoid all seeming exaggeration, we may state precisely what Logic cannot do, and what it can do, in the way of preventing us from being led astray by fallacious reasoning. It should be allowed at once that the best safeguard against error of every kind, is to be found in a sincere desire to discover the truth, which keeps the mind open to facts and arguments from whatever quarter they come—"When the eye is single the whole body is full of light." Without this, no dialectic skill can protect us from so insidious a foe as a deceitful heart. It may be farther admitted that native shrewdness can detect fallacies without the aid of logical rules. But freely granting all this, it may yet be maintained that many valuable practical as well as scientific ends are to be gained by an acquaintance with logical principles and the violations of them. It is most important, for the guidance of our thoughts, that we should know what are the essential steps involved in inference ; that we should be aware, for example, that there are always three terms, and a comparison of two of these by the third ; and that in most reasoning there is a major premiss implied in the form of a general principle. By a logical training the mind is led to look keenly into the meaning of terms and the relation of terms one to another, to place the case fairly before it, to sift the proof which may be proffered, and to determine how far it is fitted to support the conclusion. How useful, too, to know what are the common forms of invalid reasoning, to be aware of the places where error lurks, that so we may be on our guard against its insidious attacks, or ready if need be to seek it out, and expose it to view and hunt it to death. By such a discipline the mind may acquire a habit which will lead it spontaneously to reason accurately, and gender a spirit of penetration, scrutiny, and caution, which will save it from being carried along by impulse, by plausible statement and clap-trap oratory. We find the correct speaker and writer coming to speak and write accurately without construing his sentences, but it is because he has previously studied grammar ; and the arithmetician makes his calculations without referring to rules, because the habit has become part of his nature. In like manner the correct thinker can conduct a long chain of ratiocination, without thinking of syllogistic formulæ, but all the while the skill may be the result of logical training, and there may be throughout an unconscious use of the principles of reasoning. And just as an author when a dispute arises about his language, is obliged to resort to the rules of grammatical construction, and as the merchant's clerk when his accounts will not balance has to fall back on arithmetical rules to correct his blunders, so the reasoner may find it convenient when he has any cause to doubt of his own arguments, or to dispute those of his neighbor, to have logical rules ready for application. In this way, any one who has a sincere desire to discover the truth, may be guided aright in his own cogitations, and kept from aberrations on either side, and enabled to use any natural shrewdness which God may have given him, in detecting the sophistries laid in his way by others.

81. Psychology can explain how the heart sways the head. In all judgment, immediate or mediate, there is comparison; the com parison of objects, two or more, represented to the intelligence and apprehended by it. But the representation may be a misrepresentation, the apprehension a mistaken one, and the judgment become in consequence a perverted one. A prejudiced heart presents a partial, an exaggerated, a distorted case to the judicial power. This is effected through the influence of the will on the train of association. We have already noticed the fact (§ 76) that while reasoning is not the same as the association of ideas, it is yet greatly dependent on it. It is by the laws of the succession of our ideas that the notions compared are suggested. Now the will has a direct and an indirect power over the train of thought and feeling. It has a direct power in retaining the present idea, for as long as the will to retain it exists, it keeps the idea before the mind; and it is apt to detain only what pleases and gratifies vanity, pride, and passion, and it turns away from all that would reprove or humble. And then it has a more important indirect influence. In detaining the present, it collects around it a great many other thoughts connected with it by the laws of suggestion, say by the law of co-existence, or the law of correlation. In doing this, it calls into operation certain secondary laws, such as when we bestow a great amount of energy of any kind—say of thought, feeling, or attention—on any object, it will come up more frequently before the mind. The heart thus sends up to the head an immense number of ideas, all of one complexion; and the will seizes eagerly on those that please it, and as it lodges them they gather other ideas of a like description, till at last the man is bound in a fellowship from which he cannot extricate himself. This we believe to be the main source of our erroneous judgments and invalid reasonings. They spring not so much from the understanding as from the prepossessions of the heart, calling up only one kind of ideas, and tempting us to look at them exclusively and carelessly, keeping us from distinguishing between the things that differ, leading us to trace effects to wrong causes, and deceiving us by fair appearances and specious analogies.

82. Fallacies from the days of Aristotle have been logically divided into those *In Dictione* and those *Extra Dictionem*, or, to use a better mode of expression, into those in Form and those in Matter. The former are found in the very form or expression, and we need look no farther; the latter can be detected only when we look to the matter or objects of thought. Whately introduced a third division, intermediate between the two others, what he calls semi-logical, lying partly in the form, and partly in the matter. The division is a very convenient one, but cannot be consistently carried out. For Logic cannot look at mere material errors; if it did it would have to look at all errors, and therefore at all knowledge, historical, ethical, theological, scientific, practical. When confined to its proper province, it can look at mistakes only so far as they imply violations of the laws of thought. But then in order to detect them, it is often necessary to look at the matter, at least to the extent of understanding what is meant by the propositions and the argument. Fallacies of the latter kind constitute what are properly called Material fallacies, which, however, must always be logical, inasmuch as they imply a disregard of the laws of thought, but which may be more or less logical according as we have to look less or more to the matter, that is, the objects.

83. *FORMAL FALLACIES.* These can be detected

from the expression apart from the meaning or the objects. They are simply violations of the fundamental laws of reasoning, and may best be exposed by an application to them of the rules of the syllogism.

Undistributed Middle. Some one proves that Mohammed was sincere, and thence quietly infers that he was a good man. The reasoning is:

All good men are sincere;
Mohammed was sincere;
∴ Mohammed was a good man.

This violates the general rule that the middle must be distributed at least once in the premisses, which is not done here, as both premisses are affirmative with the middle term in their predicates undistributed. It also violates the special rule of the second figure, which requires one of the premisses to be negative. To legitimate the conclusion, the reasoning must take a form in which it will be at once seen that the major premiss is not true:

All sincere men are good men;
Mohammed was sincere;
∴ Mohammed was a good man.

Some one shows that religious professors have been hypocrites, and thence argues that this man who is a religious professor is a hypocrite. This conclusion is valid only when he has distributed his middle by showing that all, and not merely some, religious professors have been hypocrites.

84. *Illicit Process of Major or Minor Term.* Thus some one allows that all studies are useful which tend to prepare a man for the practical and professional duties of life, but shows that the study of Latin and Greek does not accomplish this end, and thence argues that it is useless. Put the reasoning in proper form, and it is at once seen that there is an Illicit Process of the Major, which is distributed in the conclusion and not in the premiss.

The studies which prepare for professional life are useful;
The study of Latin and Greek does not prepare for such;
∴ It is not useful.

Whatever represses the liberties of mankind is to be resisted;
Among the things which do so is government;
∴ Government is to be resisted.

Here is an illicit process of the Minor. All that we can argue is that some governments are to be resisted.

85. *Negative Premisses.* Some one is arguing against a doctrine he dislikes, and lays down a number of negative positions in the way of objection, and imagines that he has established a positive truth. Thus he shows that Christianity cannot be proven to be true by its success—for Mohammedanism succeeded; nor by its alleged miracles—for false religions have had alleged miracles. But he is not entitled thereby to draw any positive conclusion, certainly not to conclude that Christianity cannot be proven by evidence.

86. *Arguments with more than Three Terms.* Thus when it is argued, "Every one desires happiness; virtue is happiness; therefore every one desires virtue," we have no fewer than five terms: "every one," "desirous of happiness," "virtue," "happiness," "desirous of virtue." It might be possible, no doubt, to express the thought so as to exhibit only three terms; but then the fallaciousness of the whole would be evident. When it is argued that "as idolatry is a sin; and as magistrates should punish sin; so they should punish idolatry," the fallacy may be concealed by not seeing that there are more than three terms, and will at once become visible when the comparison is distinctly stated:

Sin (some sin) should be punished by magistrates;
Idolatry is a sin.

We can draw no conclusion as the middle is not distributed.

87. *Fallacies of Conditionals*, in denying the antecedent and thence denying the consequent, or affirming the consequent and thence affirming the antecedent. "Prayer may be regarded as useful, if indeed we can regard our prayers as announcing to Deity what he does not know, or changing his eternal purposes; but as we cannot tell the Omniscient what he does not already know, or change his plans, we may regard prayer as useless." Here we deny the antecedent and can draw no conclusion —as prayer may be useful on other grounds. "If this man has been much injured, he is unfit to travel; but he is unfit to travel; so he has been much injured." Here we affirm the consequent, but can thence draw no conclusion as to the antecedent, as the man may have been unfit to travel from other causes.

Fallacies in Disjunctives arise chiefly from the dividing members not making up the whole. But in order to discover this, we must look at the objects; and so this class of fallacies falls under the head of *Material.*

88. *MATERIAL FALLACIES.* All fallacies must imply a violation of the laws of thought in order to bring them within the domain of Formal Logic; but in those now to be considered we have to look to the matter in order to discover this.

AMBIGUOUS TERMS, specially AMBIGUOUS MIDDLE, in which a term is used in different senses in the premiss and conclusion, or in the middle as it appears in the two premisses. This is the Material Fallacy which approaches nearest the Formal Fallacies. In fact it falls under the head of Fallacies involving more than three terms. It is called semi-logical by Whately. It is logical in that it violates the law of thought which requires that there be only three notions compared in the three propositions. But so far as the language is concerned, there seem to be only three notions, and we have to look beyond the expression to find that under the same phrase two notions have been introduced.

89. In Part First we have dwelt at considerable length on the incidental disadvantages of language, and specially on those which spring from the ambiguity of terms. No evil would arise from the double meaning of a word provided we always had a clear apprehension of the two senses, and never slid from the one signification to the other in the course of the argument. When Paul concludes (Rom. iii. 28), that "a man is justified by faith without the deeds of the law," he is using the word 'justify' consistently throughout, as meaning 'treated by God as free from guilt.' When James says (ii. 24), "Ye see then how that by works a man is justified, and not by faith only," he too is using the phrase consistently, meaning 'seen to be just before God,' which, he says, requires the evidence of works. All candid minds will see and acknowledge that in such a case the two statements are not contradictory, and that both arguments may be conclusive. Were we steadily to bear in mind that some, as Locke and Kant, understand 'reason' as including 'reasoning,' and that others employ it to signify intuitive reason, which excludes 'reasoning,' no mischief could arise from the word having two meanings. The evil arises from the circumstance that people, both those who employ the argument and those to whom it is addressed, are apt to pass from the one sense to the other without being aware of it.

90. Paul says (Col. ii. 16), "Let no man judge you in meat, or in drink, or in respect of an holyday, or of the new moon, or of the Sabbath-days," meaning by Sabbath-day, the seventh day of the week kept at that time by many Jewish Christians. But from this some have argued that Christians are not now bound to keep the Sabbath-day, meaning the Lord's day, or first day of the week. Certain of the ancient philosophic sects of Greece, as the Stoics, laid down the general maxim, whatever is conformable to nature is virtuous and should be attended to. The Stoics approved of the principle, understanding by nature what is godlike within and without us. Bishop Butler says it can be justified only when we properly understand our nature, and give to the moral power the highest and an authoritative commanding place. But some have understood by it, all that is in our nature ; and that therefore addictedness to pleasure in youth and to gain in old age are allowable, as being agreeable to nature. Many have argued in former ages that, as a country is prosperous according to its wealth (which is true in the political-economy use of the phrase), and as a certain nation has much wealth (meaning coin or precious metals), it must therefore be in a prosperous condition. There has been a great deal of logomachy in the dispute as to whether there is a reality in heat, light, and color : some meaning by these phrases the sensation in our frame ; others, the external qualities exciting the sensation. Many are puzzled in the present day when they hear heat described as a mode of motion, understanding by heat the feeling in our organism which, they say truly, cannot be a mode of motion, whatever the exciting cause may be. There is an ambiguity in the phrases 'obliged,' 'necessitated,' which has led to false conclusions being drawn ; some understanding by the phrases an external physical compulsion, and others, a moral inclination in the will. Thus some argue that since no man has any discredit in what he is necessitated to do, and as certain men are necessitated by their nature to do base deeds, so they are not to be blamed nor punished. An unsatisfactory ethical discussion has been encouraged by the uncertain meaning of the word 'good,' which sometimes means 'morally good,' and sometimes is so widened as to include happiness. There are writers who deceive themselves as they pass from one of the meanings to the other. They show that happiness is a good thing and to be promoted, and then go on to speak of it as moral good. The words 'conceivable' and 'inconceivable' have helped much to confuse the controversy between the *a priori* and *a posteriori* philosophies. Descartes maintained that whatever is clearly and distinctly conceived, is to be at once believed; and many have argued that what is inconceivable is to be rejected. It is shown in opposition to them, that we can clearly and distinctly conceive, in the sense of picture or image, many things, such as ghosts, in the existence of which we have no faith; and that there are things, such as antipodes, which were reckoned inconceivable in one age, and believed in a later age. If the defenders of intuitive truth would not render themselves the easy prey of their opponents, they should abandon all such vague language, and show that there are truths which man perceives at once. There is a like ambiguity in the statement that all man's ideas are got by experience: it is true in the sense that experience is necessary in order to the ideas springing up; but it is not true that experience apart from an intuitive capacity, can give us such ideas as those of moral good and infinity.

91. *Fallacia Accidentis,* with its converse, *Fallacia a dicto secundum quid ad dictum simpliciter.* In both, a term is used in one of the propositions of the syllogism to signify a thing in itself, or in its substance, and in the other with certain adjuncts or accidents: as in the hackneied example, "What is bought in the market is eaten; raw meat is bought in the market; therefore it is eaten." It is thus that orators and devotees deceive others and are deceived themselves, while they use the phrases loyalty, authority, liberty, faith, religion. These are noble qualities in themselves, but men confound the accompaniments with the essence: and they commend loyalty to a person which is disloyalty to a nation; and obedience to a power which has no rightful authority; and a liberty which is licentiousness as being without law; and a faith which is credulity; and a religion which is superstition. It was thus that the cavaliers denounced the covenanters and puritans as disloyal, though no set of men ever so meant to be loyal. It is thus that some denounce as infidels all who will not understand as they do the first chapter of Genesis, or account as they do for the formation of the strata of the earth's surface, or the origin of animal species.

92. *Equivocation,* embracing in it *Amphiboly.* A member of the House of Commons was supposed to have called another member a liar, and a confused dispute arose whether that member had been called a liar, or had told a lie, when the gentleman charged rose and said solemnly, "It is quite true and I am sorry for it," meaning, "It is quite true he is a liar;" but understood, "it is quite true I said it." To this head may be referred the response of the oracle, "Aio te, Aeacida, Romanos vincere posse," and the prophecy "The Duke yet lives that Henry shall depose." But there are far worse instances of equivocation than these, in common use. A person is charged with having struck another with a stick to the danger of his life, and he replies that he did not injure him with a stick, though he is conscious all the while that he did so with a bar of iron. Or some one is charged with having done a base act on a certain day in the forenoon, and he denies it, because he did it after twelve o'clock. It is a weapon which has been employed in all ages in politics, in courtship, in commercial transactions: language is employed which is capable of being understood in a just sense, but which is meant to leave a different impression on those to whom it is addressed.

The person who resorts to these mean tricks may imagine that he is free from the sin of lying; but the fact is, his lying is of a peculiarly aggravated character, as with the falsehood there is low and deceitful cunning. Closely allied is the fallacy of what is called

93. *Oblique Expression.* It is used by the courtier and the flatterer, who keep within the limits of truth in their statement, but intend that their words should suggest much more to those whom they address. It is employed by the calumniator when he does not bring a direct accusation—which might be met; but he hints and insinuates certain dark charges fitted to raise our worst suspicions. We see it exhibited by the guilty man when he puts on a look of injured innocence; or affects a virtuous indignation because such an offence could be charged against him. There are certain speakers guilty of it in every sentence, and certain writers exhibit it in every page, for they can say nothing clearly and plainly. It has been said of Hume, as a historian, that, "without asserting much more than can be proven, he gives prominence to all the circumstances which support his case, or glides lightly over those which are unfavorable to it."

94. *FALLACIES OF CONFUSION.* Almost all paralogisms might be put under the head of Confusion of Thought. It is the office of Logic to correct error by exhibiting the various kinds of confusion into which the mind may fall in apprehending, judging, and reasoning. The phrase, Fallacy of Confusion, might be restricted to those errors which arise from confounding in our minds the nature of the notions and the relation of the notions. Thus we may be employing in argument a notion of which we have a very obscure apprehension. It is a concept, and we do not know what are the common qualities which join the objects in the concept, and in the process we suppose these qualities now to be one thing and now another. We are reasoning about the 'good,' and now we suppose it to be the morally good and now to be happiness. Or we use abstract and general terms as if they were singulars, and after making proper enough predications of them, we reach a conclusion in which they are to be understood as individual existing things. Plato is right in saying that there are ideas in and before the Divine Mind; that these Ideas exist as model forms or laws in nature; and that the human mind may rise to the contemplation of them. But he is wrong when he speaks of them as existences, like God, the world, and the human mind. Scientific men are right when they say that the planets are held in their spheres by gravitation, but they err when they give gravitation a being and a power different from the bodies themselves of which gravitation is a property. Under this head we may place the fallacy of *husteron proteron*, of *placing that which is first last*, and *last first*. The good woman mentioned in the "Guesses after Truth," had a truth in her mind, but expressed it very confusedly, when she thanked God that he had placed the Sabbath at the beginning of the week instead of the middle of it, as thereby everything was kept in order.

95. *Fallacy of Division and Composition*, in which a term is used in one judgment collectively, and in another distributively. In Division, a term is used collectively in the major premiss and distributively in the minor, and in Composition, the reverse. The liability to fall into this fallacy is much furthered by the ambiguity of the word "all," which may signify the whole collectively, or may mean every one; and we fall into a fallacy when we use it in one proposition of the syllogism in one sense, and in another proposition in the other. It is thus that when an army gains a victory, every regiment and soldier in it is apt to claim a share of the credit, though he may in no way have helped to produce the result. Many a one reasons thus:

What is no uncommon occurrence may reasonably be expected;
To be successful in play is no uncommon occurrence;
∴ To be successful in play may be reasonably expected.

This fallacy is involved in the reasoning of the youth, who says or feels:—I may lay out a certain sum on fine clothes and not be in difficulties, and a like sum in jewels and not be in debt, and as large a sum in travelling without spending all my money, and concludes that he may procure all these enjoyments. The same error is involved, but in an opposite way, when the greedy man being asked to subscribe to one charity after another, and finding that if he gives to all he will be ruined, determines to give to none. "Two distinct objects may, by being dexterously presented again and again in quick succession to the mind of a cursory reader, be so associated together in his thoughts as to be conceived capable, when in fact they are not, of being actually combined in practice. The fallacious belief thus induced, bears a striking resemblance to the optical illusion effected by that ingenious and philosophic toy called the Thaumatrope, in which two objects painted on opposite sides of a card—for instance, a man and a horse, a bird and a cage—are, by a quick rotatory motion, made to impress the eye in combination so as to form one picture, of the man on the horse's back, the bird in the cage." (Whately.)

96. *Imperfect Division.* This fallacy specially appears in Disjunctive Reasoning, in which it is implied in order to the validity of the reasoning, that the members make up the whole, and that they exclude one another. But it often happens that the parts named do not make up the whole:

If it is decreed that you will recover from this disease you do not need a physician; if it is decreed that you will not recover you do not need a physician;
But you will either recover or not recover;
∴ You do not need a physician.

Whereas there may be a third supposition; that it is decreed that you are to recover by means of a physician.

Quite as frequently the divisions are not exclusive, in other words, cross each other. In the famous controversy between the *a priori* and *a posteriori* philosophies, the supporters of the latter shut their opponents up into the dilemma, that such ideas as those of power and moral good are to be had either from some innate power exclusively or from experience, and then show that experience has to do with their formation; but the truth may be that the two combine; the native power may work in our experience, and on the occasion of our experience.*

97. We now come to consider fallacies arising, not so much from the terms, as from their relation to one another in the reasoning.

Fallacy of Shifting Ground, as when the advocate or opponent of a cause begins as if he were about to prove it to be good and right, and as he proceeds shows that some good may be derived from it; or that it is wrong and bad, and shows that it has led to certain supposed evil results. Under this head may be placed the common practice of persons professing to prove that a certain deed has been done, but dwelling chiefly on the enormity or the excellence of the deed, with the view of rousing

* Triptolemus Yellowley thought there were two ways of draining Braebaster Loch, one down the Linklater Glen, the other by the Scalmester burn. But the Udaller saw the imperfection of his division. "There is a third way; let each of us start an equal proportion of brandy, lime juice, and sugar, into the loch, and let us assemble all the jolly Udallers of the country, and in twenty-four hours you shall see dry ground where the loch of Braebaster now is."

the feelings and to prevent it being seen that they have not established their point. Francis Bacon is charged with having received an estate from his friend the Earl of Essex, and afterwards being unkind to him; and the strength of the writer is expended in dwelling on the evil of ingratitude, especially on the part of so great a man, instead of proving the alleged facts. In oral controversy how often is it found that you combat "both your opponent's premisses alternately, and shift the attack from the one to the other, without waiting to have either of them decided before you quit it. 'And besides' is an expression one may often hear from a disputant who is proceeding to a fresh argument, when he cannot establish, and yet will not abandon, his first." Under this head may be placed:

98. *Fallacia Plurium Interrogationum* consists in asking two or more questions as if they were one and the same, and when one of them is answered it is interpreted as applied to the other. It is a trick of a low kind often resorted to by lawyers in examining witnesses, with the view of puzzling them, and turning their answers to a wrong account. "You were swayed by the love of money in the transaction?" (meaning exclusively,) to which the witness answers "yes," (meaning in part.) Another question follows: "In being swayed by money you were acting selfishly in the transaction?" The fallacy appears in higher matters. Thus the utilitarian puts to us the questions: "You deny that virtue consists in utility?" "Yes." "Then you deny that utility is a good thing." The fallacy is to be met by accurately answering each question separately.

99. *PETITIO PRINCIPII*, or *BEGGING OF THE QUESTION*, "in which one of the premisses either is manifestly the same in sense with the conclusion, or is actually proved from it." A man may prove that the Bible comes from God because it contains certain elevated doctrines which could not be discovered by the natural sagacity of the writers ; but after he has done this he cannot turn round and prove that these doctrines are true because they are contained in the Bible. We ought not to prove the existence and unity of God from its being contained in Scripture, and then prove the truth of Scripture from its giving us such high views of the existence, unity, and nature of God.

100. And here it may be proper to remark that the Syllogism or Syllogistic reasoning is not, as has often been alleged, a Petitio Principii. As put in syllogistic form, the premiss does not in any sense depend on the conclusion; and the conclusion follows, not from one of the premisses, but from the two, or rather from the relations between the things compared in the premisses. It is when the relations predicated in the two propositions are brought before the mind that it sees the force of the inference.

101. *Arguing in a Circle* is the common manifestation of the Petitio Principii. The person covertly, it may be ignorantly, assumes a fact or principle, and by means of it reaches a conclusion, which he is found after a while to be employing to establish the fact or principle with which he set out. Thus we find persons arguing that their church is the true one because sanctioned by God ; and that since it is the true church, God has sanctioned it. Or they reach the truth of the Bible from the authority of the Church, and infer the authority of the Church from the Bible. A man maintains that his party is good because it promotes good measures ; and that a measure is good because promoted by his party. Malebranche is believed by many to have become involved in this circle, when he proved the existence of an external world by the authority of Scripture ; and he certainly did so, if it be impossible to establish the authority of Scripture unless you assume the existence of an external world. Much of the elaborate reasoning employed in the discussion of intricate subjects—for example, that of Spinoza in his Ethics—is a movement in a circle—like that of a man who, after toiling for hours in the dark, comes to the place from which he started. It is evident that the more involved the chain, the more difficult to detect the unsatisfactory junctions. The most effective way of exposing the whole, is to insist on narrowing the circle, and so spreading out the links that we may see the feeble place, where the conclusion is employed to support the premiss, and the whole chain made to hang on nothing.

102. *IGNORATIO ELENCHI*, or *IRRELEVANT CONCLUSION.* Logicians suppose that in discussion the opponent should prove the elenchus or contradictory of your doctrine; and when he fails to do this, and establishes a different proposition, he is said to be guilty of an Ignoratio Elenchi. But the language may be so widened as to include under it all cases of Irrelevant Conclusion—that is, in which persons establish, not the conclusion which they ought, but another which may be mistaken for it. The dispute is, whether any one has a right to compel a father to educate his child in a way different from what he is doing, in religion or in something else, and one of the disputants thinks he has settled the whole question when he has shown that the father is educating his child wrong. Locke in showing that the syllogism is of little or no value, proves that man can reason without the use of syllogisms. "There are many men that reason exceeding clear and rightly, who know not how to make a syllogism." "God has not been so sparing to men to make them barely two-legged creatures, and left it to Aristotle to make them rational." Macaulay in his Article on Bacon, thinks he has proven that a knowledge of the canons of induction is of little use, since men, without knowing them, are practising them from morning to night. Under this general head may be placed several other fallacies.

103. *The Fallacy of proving only Part of the Question.* As when a man is charged with murder, and the prosecutor proves that he killed a man. The judge and jury will insist that it be farther shown that he did the deed, not in self-defence, or from provocation at the moment, but with malicious intent. A person is denounced as a liar, and his accuser when asked for his evidence shows that he did make certain misstatements, it may be from misapprehension or misinformation. When the agriculturist objected to the Shetland plough with only one handle, Magnus Troil proved part of his point when he replied, "Tell me how it were possible for Neil of Lupness, that lost one arm by his fall from the crag of Nekbrekan, to manage a plough with two handles?"

104. *Fallacy of Objections,* that of concluding that a proposal is to be set aside because there are objections to it—as if the captiousness of men were not prepared to object to anything, even to the existence and worship of God. It is not enough to show that there are objections; it must be shown that there are stronger reasons against it, than for it. Thus in one of the rising questions of the day, when it is proposed to appoint young men to public offices by competitive examination, an opponent thinks it sufficient to object that at times you might thus get a person who has no great business capacity; whereas it properly devolves on him to show that by this mode of appointment you would not get young men of such high business talents and character as by the method now practised of political patronage.

105. *Argumentum ad Hominem.* As all reasoning is *ex concessis,* we are entitled in reasoning with any one to proceed on the principles avowed by him, though these might not just be the principles to which we might appeal in dealing with others or with mankind generally. Our Lord often employed this method in dealing with the cavils of the Pharisees. The argument, however, will not be acknowledged as valid by those who do not admit the principles on which it proceeds. That loose appeal made to faith in the last age by so many German and British writers, is not allowed to be legitimate by those who insist on your proving by the proper tests that a faith must be intuitive, or that it is supported by sufficient mediate evidence, before they are inclined to yield to it. It is not an honest use of the *argumentum ad hominem,* when we take advantage of premisses which those with whom we are arguing allow, but which we do not ourselves believe, —except, indeed, when our aim is simply to make them doubt of their premisses by showing the consequences to which they lead.

106. *Argumentum ad Populum,* or an appeal to principles cherished by the great body of the people. It is allowable only when the principles are right and proper in themselves, and are conscientiously entertained by those who advocate them. It is not legitimate when they are wrong in themselves, or when he who urges them is doing so hypocritically. It will commonly happen in the end that such a deceitful use of the argument will turn against the person employing it. In no case is it allowable to employ this argument to stir up a malignant spirit or violent acts.

107. *Argumentum ad Verecundiam.* It consists of an appeal to antiquity, to the opinions of ancestors, to the religion of the country. This line of argument may prove that we are not rashly to disturb the established order of things ; but it goes no farther. It does not tend to prove, that if we are constrained otherwise by truth or by duty, we must believe as our forefathers did, or decline to disturb the present order of things.

108. *Argumentum ad Ignorantiam,* as when you insist on a man believing a thing because he knows nothing to the contrary. It is thus that people have been frightened by horrid pictures, drawn by priests or pretenders, of the world to come. It is thus that some would have us believe in animal magnetism, in clairvoyance, and the like, because they exhibit phenomena which we cannot explain. The legitimate conclusion in such cases is, that we should suspend our judgment, and wait for light to come from true religion, or scientific research.

109. *Fallacy of Pretension.* We are inclined to introduce some such head as this, to include certain very common cases of wrong inference. It would embrace, for instance, the Fallacy of References, in which there is an appeal by authors or speakers to passages or to authorities which are not expected to be very narrowly searched, or which, if narrowly scrutinized, do not bear out the conclusion. It is thus that Buckle, in his work on Civilization, has deceived (we do not say intentionally) many by numerous quotations which, if narrowly sifted in their historical connection, are not fitted to bear up all that he would rear on them. It is thus that a dogmatic air overawes many who are not inclined to think for themselves or institute an independent inquiry. Many feel as if such men as Hobbes and Comte must be speaking truly and with a profound knowledge of their subject, when they utter their statements so clearly and so confidently—whereas all this may have arisen from their never having looked at anything more than one side of a very complex question. Under this head we place the *Idola Theatri* of Bacon, or the deceiving influence exercised by great doctors, heads of sects, and leaders of opinion.

110. *Argument from Consequences.* This is allowable in questions of pure expediency, as, for example, in considering a proposal to pass a law for the suppression of intemperance, or gambling, or licentiousness; we ought to inquire whether it would effect the end in view. But when the question is one of truth or right, we should not in the first instance appeal to results. There is a constant tendency on the part of some, when a new scientific truth is divulged, to reject it because it may produce evil consequences by undermining religious beliefs, or good social sentiments. But if a doctrine be true, and a deed be right, the consequences must be good whether we see it or not. After we have established the truth or falsehood of a doctrine on independent evidence, then we may allowably trace the consequences—always, however, in a spirit of candor and fairness.

111. *Mistakes as to the Onus Probandi.* When any one makes a positive affirmation, the Burden of Proof undoubtedly lies on him, and his evidence should be such as can stand the laws of evidence in the particular department. If it be a mathematical truth, he must demonstrate it by principles self-evident, necessary, universal. If it be a scientific truth, he should bring evidence that can stand the tests of the canons of induction. If it be a historical event, he must show that it can stand the tests of historical criticism. If it be reached by deduction, it may be tried by the syllogism. But if he has failed to give sufficient proof, he is not entitled to insist on those who may not give in to his affirmation, proving the contradictory of it. They may very properly content themselves with suspending their judgment till proof is adduced. For example, if a man says a particular plant is to be found in a certain country—say azaleas in Scotland—we expect him to produce the plant. But he is not entitled to demand of us that we go round the whole country and show that there is no such plant. It is often easy to disprove a general statement by an individual case. If a man were to say that all the blessings which God sends are universal or common to the whole race, you could confute him by showing (in the third figure of the syllogism) that certain blessings, such as the means of education, had not been placed within the power of all mankind. But to prove a general negative is often difficult or impossible ; for you would have to go round all possible cases, and show that no one of them admits of a positive affirmation being made regarding it.

112. We now come to consider certain Fallacies usually treated of in works of Formal Logic, but conducting us into Particular or Objective Logic, which looks at thought as directed to special classes of objects. No doubt there are violations of the laws of discursive thought involved, but in order to find out what they are, and how they are to be remedied, we must go to other departments of knowledge.

Fallacies of Analogy. By analogy we are to understand, not the resemblance of one thing to another, but the resemblance of ratios or relations. Thus the sovereign of a country is said, by analogy, to be the head of the country, because he bears the same relation to the country as the head does to the body. Two fallacies may spring from the use or abuse of analogies. First we may suppose that the things related resemble each other because their relations do. The wing of a bird and the wing of a butterfly are said by naturalists to be analogous, for they serve the same purpose, that of flight ; but the two members do not resemble each other in their structure. We are exhorted by our Lord in praying to God, to imitate the importunity of the woman who continued to apply to the judge till she gained her case ; but we are not to understand that God resembles that judge in character, or the motives by which he is swayed. Another fallacy arises from carrying the analogy too far. Thus some have argued that since all nations resemble animals, in having a period of childhood, youth, and maturity, they will therefore resemble them in having a time of decreptitude and death—whereas there may be causes at work in certain nations, such as education and Christianity, which will save them from the latter stages. The argument from Analogy is : " Things resemble each other in certain known respects ; they will therefore resemble each in certain other and unknown respects." This is an argument which is often conclusive. Thus the connoisseur argues : this painting resembles the paintings of Rubens in certain characteristic marks, and must resemble them in this respect also, that it has been produced by the same hand. Thus it is that the anatomist finding one fossil hind leg of an animal, concludes that the other must have been like it. It is in a great measure by this principle that the palæontologist can construct the whole animal from a few bones found in the dust of the earth. It is the province of Inductive Logic to lay down some rule to guide us as to when the conclusion is valid, and when it is invalid. Formal Logic can assist us no way at this place. All that it can do is to show where error may lurk, and insist on our seeking to obtain some general principle (as a major) to guide and guard us.

113. *Imperfect Enumeration.* In all departments of science and practical knowledge, general laws are gained by the observation of particular facts. But what number and what kind of observations are sufficient to entitle us to declare that we have discovered the law? A sailor reasons : 'Three times did I set sail on a Friday, and in each of the voyages I encountered a storm ; it is clear that Friday is an unlucky day.' Another met once or twice with a calamity after sitting at a table where there was a company numbering thirteen, and resolves always to leave a company when he discovers it to be composed of this number. A third met with calamities on several occasions when he persevered in a journey after a hare had crossed his path, and he now turns back whenever that animal crosses the road on which he is travelling. Every enlightened man sees that these are cases of narrow enumeration. But what is a sufficient enumeration? It can easily be shown that the sufficiency does not depend on the number of the cases. Mr. Mill puts the question: "Why is a single instance in some cases sufficient for a complete induction, while in others myriads of concurring instances, without a single exception known or presumed, go such a very little way towards establishing a universal proposition?" and declares that he who will answer this question is wiser than the ancients. Bacon, followed by Sir J. Herschell, Mr. Mill, and others, have tried to answer it by means of Prerogative Instances (§ 71) and Canons of Induction, and have been so far successful. The Logic of Induction is seeking to lay down principles which may decide for us when we have such an enumeration as to authorize us to say that we have reached a law. But Formal Logic can do nothing more than warn us against trusting in imperfect enumerations, and require us to look out for some principle to authorize the conclusion we would draw.

114. *Non Causa pro Causa.* The inquiry into Causes is not the same as the inquiry into Laws, referred to in last section. In the inquiry into Laws, we are seeking a mere co-ordination of facts; in the inquiry into Causes we are seeking after antecedent agents having a producing power. The one inquiry, as well as the other, carries us beyond Formal Logic into Inductive Logic, and indeed into the Natural Sciences which treat of objects. Formal Logic, however, can guard us against certain errors, and draw our attention to some important distinctions.

115. *Post Hoc ergo propter Hoc.* A remarkable meteor was seen in the sky, and followed by a dreadful national calamity: a conjunction among the planets was followed by a royal marriage which issued in far-reaching conse-

13

quences; and the superstitious conclude that one of the facts had some kind of causal connection with the other. We have outlived these weaknesses of past ages: but we have not outgrown the fallacies on which they proceeded. A country or college has prospered under a certain government or management, and some conclude that it was because of the government or management, and oppose all projected improvements.

116. *Fallacy of mistaking Sign for Cause.* The quack doctor falls into this, when on seeing certain spots on the body he attacks and removes them, thereby, it may be, sending the malady farther into the frame, instead of curing it in its seat. The quack statesman is guilty of the same error, when discovering the existence of ignorance and crime in a country he contents himself with punishing them, instead of trying to remove the deep moral causes from which they spring. Buckle has, as it appears to us, fallen into the fallacy; he traces all civilization to mere intellectual power, excluding moral causes: whereas the intellect in many cases, as in Scotland and the United States, was awakened by moral causes of which the intellectual life was, properly speaking, the effect.

117. In order to keep us from falling under the power of these fallacies, Logic calls our attention to two important distinctions. There is the distinction between the *Causa Essendi* and the *Causa Cognoscendi.* The former is the objective cause in the powers of nature or of God; the latter, the facts or means by which we come to know the objective cause of the occurrence. The two are often confounded by much the same language being employed by us to denote them. Thus we speak of the ground being wet because it has rained; and of its having been rain because the ground is wet. It is evident that the *Causa Cognoscendi* is often an effect indicating the *Causa Essendi;* thus the melting of snow may be a proof or a sign of the rise of temperature which has made the snow to melt. Of very much the same character is the distinction between REASON and CAUSE; the Reason being that which brings conviction to us, and the Cause that which produces the phenomenon. The increase of temperature is the cause of the melting of the snow, but the melting of the snow as being an effect may, on being contemplated by us, be the means of revealing the action of the Cause.

FUNDAMENTAL LAWS OF DISCURSIVE THOUGHT.

118. It now only remains to try to enunciate the fundamental laws which lie at the basis of all Logical operations. These work in our minds without our being conscious of them—we are as little conscious of them, as we are of the physiological laws involved in our breathing. We can discover them only by careful observation and analytic generalization of the operations of discursive thought. A knowledge of them does not assist us in spontaneous reasoning, but it is of great value to all who would reflectively acquaint themselves with the processes of thinking. They are such as the following:

119. I. THE LAW OF IDENTITY, which may be expressed, "the same is the same, perceived it may be at different times and with different concomitants." This rules all cases in which we draw an affirmative proposition from a proposition or propositions, in which the relation of the two terms is one of identity. Thus it being given that "Jonathan Edwards is the greatest American metaphysician," we get the Implied Judgment "the greatest American metaphysician was Jonathan Edwards;" or, it being farther allowed that "Jonathan Edwards was the

Missionary to the Indians at Stockbridge," we get by reasoning the Conclusion that "the Missionary to the Indians at Stockbridge, was the greatest American metaphysician."

120. II. The Law of Contradiction. This law is "it is impossible for the same thing to be and not to be at the same time." Or bringing out a farther aspect of the same truth, it may take the form: "A thing cannot have, and not have, the same attribute at the same time." It rules in all cases in which we get a negative proposition from a negative proposition by implication, or from negative propositions by reasoning, as when it is given us that, "Francis Bacon is not the same as Roger Bacon," we say that "Roger Bacon was not the same as Francis Bacon," or, with another proposition allowed, that "Francis Bacon was the expounder of the Inductive Method," so "Roger Bacon was not the expounder of the Inductive Method."

121. III. The Law of Excluded Middle, Lex Exclusi Tertii aut Medii; that is, either a given judgment is true, or its contradictory—there is no middle course or third supposition. Thus it must either be true or not true that "God exists;" and it must either be true or false that "this man was ignorant of the deed;" and if it can be shown that he was not ignorant of it, you cannot look upon him as if he was ignorant.

122. IV. The Principle of Equality, "things which are equal to the same things, are equal to one another." It is thus we argue that $2 + 2 = 4$; and $2 \times 2 = 4$; therefore $2 + 2 = 2 \times 2$.

In all cases in which the propositions are Equivalent (P. II., § 14), these are the sole regulating principles. But where the propositions imply Extension and Comprehension, other Laws come in and act along with these.

123. V. The Dictum of Aristotle, "whatever is predicated of a Class Notion, may be predicated of all that is contained in it." This is seen to be true on the bare contemplation of the nature, of the extension, of a concept. Combine this principle with that of Identity, and we get Affirmative Judgments implied or inferred. Thus as "all plants die," so "some plants die," and as "Coniferæ are plants," so "Coniferæ die." Combine this principle with that of Contradiction, and we draw negative propositions. As "no men are perfect," so "some men are not perfect," and "the Greeks" "who were some men," "were not perfect." These principles, the Dictum combined with the Law of Identity in affirmatives, and of Contradiction in negatives, rule all ordinary syllogistic and conditional reasoning.

Combine the Dictum with the principle of Excluded Middle, and we get a number of Implied Judgments. Thus we argue that if it be false that "no metal is heavier than water," it must be true that "some metals are heavier than water." *Reductio per Impossibile* (P. III., § 40), proceeds on these two principles.

124. VI. THE PRINCIPLES OF ATTRIBUTION, "every attribute implies a thing of which it is an attribute." Or, it may take a subordinate form, "All that is in an attribute is in the thing that contains the attribute," or, as Leibnitz expresses it, "Nota notæ est nota rei ipsius." This law has a place in Abstraction (P. I., § 11); in Immediate Inferences from Privative Conceptions (P. II., § 49), and in all reasoning in Comprehension (P. III., § 42), that is, reasoning in which we specially look at the attributes. Thus we argue that as intelligence, conscience, and free will, make the beings who possess them moral and responsible agents, so man, as possessing these, must be regarded as a moral and responsible agent.

125. VII. THE LAW OF DIVISION, "the dividing members make up the whole class." This is the principle—always along with the Dictum—regulating Disjunctive Reasoning, as when we argue that if a man has not taken two of three possible roads, he must have taken the third. Combined with the principle of Excluded Middle, it regulates reasoning in which we argue on the supposition that the members exclude one another. "If this man must be either a fool or a knave," it follows if he is not a fool, "he must be a knave."

126. VIII. THE PRINCIPLES OF WHOLE AND PARTS. "What is true of the whole is true of each of the parts." This holds good of parts whether they be sub-classes or attributes. This principle helps to guide us in Subalternation, and in all reasoning involving Extension and Comprehension. Another Principle to be placed under the same head is, "The parts make up the whole;" a principle involved in all reasoning which proceeds on the completeness of Division.

127. In looking at the discursive operations of the mind, we have constantly come to such principles as these. The consideration, however, belongs not to Logic, but to Metaphysics (P. I., § 1), or the science of First or Fundamental truths. The author of this treatise has treated of them, of their nature and mode of development, in the *Intuitions of the Mind Inductively Investigated.* He has there shown that such principles are Intuitive, that is, are seen to be true at once; and this not by any form in the mind, but by the capacity which the mind has to contemplate objects, and by the exercise of that capacity in looking at objects. He has shown that the Law is not consciously before the mind when it is exercising it, and that it is in looking at an individual object, or judgment, that it is called forth. The mind has not consciously before it the Law of Equality when it declares that if A is equal to B, and B to C, then A must be equal to C. It reaches the conclusion at once on the contemplation of the equal lines. The Law of Equality is discovered by us by a generalization of the individual judgments.

APPENDIX.

I.—EXERCISES AS TO FORMS.

The Notion.

1. Are the following Singulars, Abstracts, or Universals, and if Universals, are they Generalized Abstracts or Generalized Concretes, viz.: Aristotle, Rationality, Rational, Man, Beauty, Good, The Good, Homeless, The Creator, Creature, Resolute, Plant, Mammal, Substance, Mind ?

What sort of terms are the following, viz.: Multitude, This Regiment, David King of Israel, The First King of Rome, The greatest living Sculptor, The Dog Cesar, This Dog, That Bird-Flying, The most distinguished Soldier in the Army, Husband, Husband and Wife,

> "The glass of fashion and the mould of form,
> The observed of all observers."

2. What are the Terms in the following, and what sort of Terms ? "Thou (Falstaff) didst swear to me upon a parcel gilt goblet, setting in my Dolphin Chamber, at the round table, by a sea-coal fire, upon Wednesday in Whitsunweek, when the prince broke thy head for liking his father to a singing man of Windsor; thou didst swear to me then, as I was washing thy wound, to marry me and make me my lady thy wife. Canst thou deny it ? Did not good wife Keech, the butcher's wife, come and call me Gossip Quickly ? Coming in to borrow a mess of vinegar; telling me she had a good dish of prawns, whereby thou didst desire to eat some; whereby I told thee they were ill for a green wound ? And didst thou not, when she was gone down stairs, desire me to be no more so familiarity with such poor people, saying, that ere long they would call me madam."

"Because A F is equal to A G, and A B to A C, the two sides F A, A C are equal to the two G A, A B, each to each; and they contain the angle F A G common to the two triangles A F C, A G B; therefore the base F C is equal to the base G B, and the triangle A F C to the triangle A G B; and the remaining angles of the one are equal to the remaining angles of the other, each to each, to which the equal sides are opposite, viz.: the angle A C F to the angle A B G, and the angle A F C to the angle A G B," &c.

"To be, or not to be, that is the question;
Whether 'tis nobler in the mind to suffer
The stings and arrows of outrageous fortune,
Or to take arms against a sea of troubles,
And, by opposing, end them? To die—to sleep—
No more: and, by a sleep, to say we end
The heart-ache and the thousand natural shocks
That flesh is heir to—'tis a consummation
Devoutly to be wished. To die? to sleep?
To sleep—perchance to dream; aye, there's the rub,
For in that sleep of death what dreams may come,
When we have shuffled off this mortal coil,
Must make us pause."

3. Are the following pairs of Notions Contrary or Contradictory, viz.: Sweet and Bitter, Organic and Inorganic, Greek and Barbarian, Wise and Foolish, Animate and Inanimate, Finite and Infinite, Alive and Dead, Short or Long, Existent and Non-existent?

4. What sort of reality is there in the following, viz.: Popularity, The Rose Tribe of Plants, Gravitation, The Vine, Love of Fame, Imagination, Roman Citizen, Heat, Cold, Blue, Substance, Body?

5. Logically Define Notion, Percept, Abstract, Concept, Genus, Species, Differentia, Judgment, Equivalent Proposition, Attributive Proposition, Conditional Proposition, Disjunctive Proposition, Implied Judgments, Conditional Reasoning, Disjunctive Reasoning, Reasoning in Comprehension, Sorites, Fallacy, Ambiguous Middle, Petitio Principii, Irrelevant Conclusion.

6. Logically divide and subdivide Notion, Judgment, Reasoning, Fallacy.

7. Analyze General Notion, Collective Notion, Judgment, Argument, A Horse Galloping, Unappeasable Revenge, Remorse of Conscience.

JUDGMENT.

8. Point out Subject and Predicate and designate the Quality and Quantity of following, viz.:

A soft answer turneth away wrath.
The man's heart is not in the right place.
Dogs bark.
Great is the work of life.
Sailors are needed for the vessel.
It is wrong to put an innocent man to death.
It is the duty of every man to fear God and honor the king.
Man is capable of living in a greater variety of climates than any of the lower animals.
There was no possibility of substantiating the allegations.
The evidence proves that Phalaris was not the author of the Epistles.
Few patriots have been disinterested.
All gold mines cannot be wrought with profit.
The eagle lost much time when he submitted to learn of the crow.
The English can scarcely be said to be humble-minded.
Nothing is so easy as to object.
"In jewels and gold men cannot grow old."
There is no place like home.
None but the brave deserve the fair.
None but whites are civilized.

9. What is the Nature of the Terms in the following? Are the Propositions Equivalent or Attributive?

The crocodile is a reptile.
Alexander was a great conqueror.
Alexander was the greatest conqueror of antiquity.
Logic is the science of the Laws of Discursive Thought.
" The most sublime act is to put another before thee."
$3 \times 3 = 9$.
If the clouds rise from the hill-top it will be a fine day.
If $A = B$ then $C = D$.
The event must have occurred either on Saturday or Sunday.

"Man is endowed with the capacity of laughter." Under what head of Predicables would this be put by Aristotle? By Porphyry? And in this Treatise?

10. Convert the following:

Every circle is a conic section.
Two straight lines cannot enclose a space.
No brutes are responsible.
Some students are diligent.
Some students do not fail in anything.
Perseverance is a condition of success.
Perseverance is the condition of success.
Washington was the first American President.

11. Put the following in the forms of Opposition:

The Duke of Wellington was the conqueror at Waterloo.
Dogs bark and bite.

What are the Contradictories?

12. Interpret the following as to Denomination, Extension, and Comprehension:

Man is fallible.
David was the sweet Psalmist of Israel.
The man who slanders his neighbor is not innocent.

13. What Implied Judgments can be derived from "Benevolent actions are commendable."

14. Put the following in correct form as a Conditional, and indicate the Terms, the Antecedent, and Consequent: "This patient will recover if he takes care of himself." Put it in Categorical Form, and indicate the Subject and Predicate.

REASONING.

15. Examine the following, and say if they are valid; and if so, according to what principle:

David was the youngest son of Jesse;
David was the youth who slew Goliath;
∴ The youngest son of Jesse was the youth who slew Goliath.

Logic is the Science of the Laws of Discursive Thought;
Metaphysics is not the Science of the Laws of Discursive Thought;
∴ Logic is not Metaphysics.

16. Put the following in Syllogistic Form; indicate the Major, Minor and Middle Terms; the Major, Middle and Minor Premisses, and the Mood and Figure:

No one is free who is enslaved by his appetites; a sensualist is enslaved by his appetites; therefore a sensualist is not free.

Heavy dews fell last night and so it has not been cloudy.

From the case of the soul and body we see that there are some things to be believed which cannot be comprehended.

17. Supply the wanting proposition in the following:

No branch of science has reached perfection;
All branches of science deserve to be cultivated.
∴ . . . .

All horned animals are ruminant,
. . . .
∴ The elk is ruminant.

. . . .
The adaptation in the shoulder-joint is effected;
∴ It must have had a cause.

18. Put the following in Syllogistic Form, supplying Premisses when necessary, and indicating Mood and Figure:

When Columbus was sailing the ocean in search of a new world, he fell in with a flock of land birds and concluded that he could not be far from land.

It has been argued by some that electricity is the agent by which the nerves act upon the muscles. But that this is not the case appears from the fact that electricity may be transmitted along a nervous trunk when a string is tied lightly round it; while the passage of ordinary nervous power is as completely checked by this process as if the nerve had been divided.

His imbecility of character might have been inferred from his proneness to favorites; for all weak princes have this failing.

"Suppose ye that these Galilæans were sinners above all the Galilæans because they suffered such things."

The Scriptures cannot come from God because they contain some things which cannot be comprehended by man.

That persons may reason without language is proven by the circumstance that infants reason and yet have no language.

Bolingbroke, in arguing against the truth of the Christian religion, shows that the Christian religion has bred contentions. Burke answered him by showing that civil government had bred contentions.

'The barbarians of the isle of Melita, when they saw the venomous beast hang on Paul's hand, said among themselves, No doubt this man is a murderer, whom though he hath escaped the sea, vengeance suffereth not to live. Howbeit, they looked when he should have swollen or fallen down dead; but after they had looked a great while and saw no harm in him, they changed their mind and said, he is a god."

The dervis who told the merchants that they had lost a camel, blind in his right eye, lame in his left leg, without a front tooth, loaded with honey on one side and wheat on the other, describes the steps which had passed through his mind, "I knew that I had crossed the track of a camel which had strayed from its owner, because I saw no mark of human footsteps on the same route; I knew that the animal was blind in one eye, because it had cropped the herbage only on one side of its path; and I perceived that it was lame in one leg from the faint impression that particular foot had produced on the sand; I concluded that the animal had lost one tooth, because wherever it had grazed a small tuft of herbage was left uninjured in the centre of its bite," etc.

If it can be shown that there are two or more persons, it follows that all is not one, that all is not God. According to every scheme of pantheism, I, as part of the universe, am part of God, part of the whole which constitutes God. In all consciousness of self we know ourselves as persons; in all knowledge of other objects.

we know them as different from ourselves and ourselves as different from them. God then must be different from one part of his works. He must be different from me.

19. If the Major Term be the Predicate of the Major Proposition, prove that the Minor Premiss must be Affirmative. In what Figures does this happen?

Prove that it renders the Conclusion necessarily Universal in the First Figure, and necessarily Particular in the Third Figure.

If the Middle Term be the Predicate of both Premisses, prove that one of the Premisses must be negative.

Given the Minor Term the Predicate of Minor Premiss, prove that A cannot be a Conclusion.

Given the Major Term the Subject of Major Premiss, prove that A cannot be a conclusion.

Prove that A can be drawn only in the First Figure.

Prove that the Minor Premiss cannot be Negative in First and Third Figures.

If the Minor Premiss be E or O, the Major must be Universal.

Given I as the Major Premiss, determine the Mood and Figure.

Prove that O cannot be a Premiss in First Figure; that it cannot be the Major in the Second Figure; or the Minor in the Third Figure; and that it cannot be a Premiss in the Fourth.

20. Reduce the following to First Figure:

Every virtue promotes the general happiness;
Cunning does not promote the general happiness;
∴ Cunning is not a virtue.

All men are liable to sorrow;
Some men are in the enjoyment of great prosperity;
∴ Some in the enjoyment of great prosperity are liable to suffering.

All men are sinners;
Some men are not cruel;
∴ Some not cruel are sinners.

Every liar is mean;
No mean man should have a public office;
∴ No man should be elected to public office who is a liar.

21. Put the following in the form both of Extension and Comprehension:

Deceit, being a sin, will be detected and punished.

Cause and effect, not being a law of Discursive Thought, does not come within the province of Logic.

22. Psychology, Logic, Ethics, Æsthetics, all tend to give a power of internal observation and of analysis to the student; and these being all the mental sciences, we may conclude that all the mental sciences tend to give a power of internal observation and analysis.

Oxygen, chlorine and steam, etc., are all the gases; and as they are elastic, it follows that all the gases are elastic.

23. Dr. Reid says, "This simple reasoning, A is equal to B, and B to C, therefore A is equal to C, cannot be brought into any syllogism in mood and figure."

The narrative is trustworthy because the author has means of knowing about what he writes, and trustworthy authors must have means of knowing about what they write; the narrative is trustworthy because it is evidently sincere and candid, and trustworthy writers are sincere and candid; the narrative is consistent, and trustworthy narratives are consistent.

24. Elephants are stronger than horses;
Horses are stronger than men;
∴ Elephants are stronger than horses.

A is greater than B, and B than C, therefore A is greater than C.

Plato lived after Socrates, and Aristotle after Plato, and so Aristotle lived after Socrates.

Three-fourths of the fruit in the garden were apples;
Three-fourths of the fruit were blown down;
∴ Some of the fruit blown down were apples.

25. The fact that I defended him is a proof that I held him innocent (stated both as Conditional and Categorical).

When about to prove the equality of two given Figures, Euclid shows that if the one is not equal to the other, it must either be greater or less; and he points out the absurdity of both these suppositions:

It is known that a rider proceeding along a road and coming to a place where other three roads meet, must have taken one or other of the three; we examine two of them, and find that he had not gone by them, and we at once conclude that he must have gone on the third.

If a man is not a brute or a divinity, he is capable of making progress.

26. Put the following in form of Sorites and draw it out in a series of Syllogisms:

A demagogue must hold the populace in contempt; for being a favorite with the populace, he must know how to manage them, and in doing so he understands their weaknesses, and understanding these must hold them in contempt.

II.—EXERCISES AS TO VIOLATIONS OF THE LAWS OF THOUGHT.

IN NOTIONS.

27. Examine the following:

A line is said to have length without breadth. There can be no such line; it is a mere abstraction, a ghost, a nonentity; and all that is demonstrated regarding it can have no objective value.

"What follows from a definition follows in reality from an implied assumption, that there exists a real thing conformable thereto. This assumption in the case of the definitions of geometry is false. There exist no real things exactly conformable to the definition. There exist no points without magnitude, no lines without breadth and perfectly straight, no circles with all their radii exactly equal, nor squares with all their angles perfectly right."

"Concreta vere res sint: abstracta non sunt res sed rerum modi; modi antem nihil aliud sunt quam relationes rei ad intellectum" (Leibnitz).

"A concept cannot in itself be depicted to sense or imagination."

28. Universals have an existence prior to things and above things.

The One, the Good, are the highest realities, are the only realities, and the mind is in its highest exercise when it is contemplating them.

29. Try the following by the Rules of Definition, and amend:

A square is a four-sided figure.

(*Amended*) A square is a four-sided rectilinear figure with its sides equal.

A deer is an animal with branching horns.

The judicial power is not the legislative.

A newspaper is a printed paper appearing periodically.

Words are the signs of thought.

A general notion is an inadequate notion of an individual.

Judgment compares notions.

Conversion is the changing of terms in a proposition.

Opposed propositions are those which differ in quantity and quality.

Contradictory opposition is the opposition of contradictories.

A conditional proposition consists of two categorical propositions connected with each other.

A disjunctive proposition consists of two or more categoricals connected by the prepositions either and or.

Reasoning is the deriving of one truth from another.

A fallacy is an unsound mode of arguing.

Ambiguous middle is a fallacy in which the terms admit of more than one meaning.

Ignoratio Elenchi is drawing a wrong conclusion.

Petitio Principii is a begging of the question.

30. Try the following by the Rules of Division:

Discursive Thought may be divided into the Term, Judgment, and Syllogism.

Animals may be divided into Quadrupeds, Birds, Fishes, Reptiles, and Invertebrata.

Literature consists of History, Biography, Tales, Theology, Poetry.

Notions are Concrete, Singular, and Universal.

Propositions are Affirmative, Negative, Universal.

All our ideas must be had either from Experience or *a priori*.

31. Analyze Pleasure, the Sensation of Heat, the Idea of the Color White, Consciousness.

In Judgments.

32. Criticise the following: "Every notion holding the place of a predicate in a proposition must have a determinate quantity in thought." "The relation between the terms of a proposition is one not only of similarity, but of identity." "The terms of a proposition are of an absolute equality, and all propositions an equation of subject and predicate."

33. What is conducive to happiness is good, and so
The good is that which is conducive to happiness.
All equilateral triangles are equiangular, and therefore
All equiangular triangles are equilateral.
That God is infinite implies that the Infinite is God.
We are not entitled to say that because Raphael was the greatest painter which Italy has produced, that therefore the greatest painter which Italy has produced was Raphael; but simply that among the greatest painters which Italy has produced was Raphael.

34. Since it is false that all men are liars, its contrary must be true, that no men are liars.
Since it is true that some men are very designing, it cannot be true that some men are not designing.

35. If Alexander was the son of Philip, we can surely argue by Immediate Inference that Philip was the father of Alexander.

In Reasoning.

36. Are the following allowable, E A I, A E I, E A E? Is A A I admissible in Fig. I.? Or I A I or A E E? In what Figures are A A I and I A I admissible?

37. Why is I E O to be rejected? A person urged that there might be a valid syllogism in I E O, and gave the following:

I Some X is Y;
E Every Y is not Z;
O Some X is not Z.

38. All wise legislators suit their laws to the genius of their nation;
Lycurgus did so;
∴ Lycurgus was a wise legislator.

Whatever is universally believed must be true;
The existence of God is not universally believed;
∴ It cannot be true.

Cloven feet being found universally in horned animals, we may conclude that this fossil animal, since it appears to have had cloven feet, was horned.

He must be an atheist, for all atheists hold these opinions.

You see that men who are indifferent to all religion do not seek to compel others to believe as they do; and as this man does not seek to compel others to believe as he does, we may conclude that he is indifferent to religion.

39. Liberty is a good thing, provided it is not abused; but it is abused, so it is not a good thing.

All those who say that Logic can teach man to reason must approve of Logic; but as you cannot say that Logic teaches man to reason, you cannot approve of it.

This world would be a happy one if all men were good; but all men are not good, so our world is not a happy one.

40. Examine the following, both as Categoricals and Conditionals:

All must approve of this student who consider him diligent; and as you approve of him, you must consider him diligent.

There is always discontent in a country when it is ill-governed; and as there is always discontent in Ireland, we may conclude that it is ill-governed.

Provided the differences between one political party and another, and one religious sect and another, are of no moment, they ought to tolerate each other: but the differences are important, so they ought not to tolerate each other.

41. Honors and rewards by the government or private patrons are useless; they cannot influence the stupid, and men of genius rise above them.

There is and can be no revelation of His Will by God: for if the matter of it cannot be received and comprehended by the human faculties, it is no revelation; and if, on the other hand, it can be compassed and comprehended by the human faculties, it could be attained by them, and is no revelation.

42. If it be a good thing to have faith, surely he who believes in the Koran has faith, and must have a good thing.

It is absurd to maintain that when we cannot avoid thinking or conceiving of a thing, it must be true; for some persons cannot be in darkness without thinking of ghosts, in which they do not believe.

43. I think the government should punish this man, as he has told a flagrant falsehood, which is wrong, and he who does wrong deserves to be punished, and government is appointed for the punishment of evil doers.

44. The Irish are witty, and this man being an Irishman, must be witty.

Epimenides the Cretan says, that "all the Cretans are liars;" but Epimenides is himself a Cretan: therefore he is himself a liar. But if he be a liar, what he says is untrue, and consequently the Cretans are veracious: but Epimenides is a Cretan, and therefore what he says is true.

If I buy this piece of land it will be profitable; if I engage in this mercantile speculation it will be profitable; if I buy this house it will be profitable; and so I may do all these and find it profitable.

To lay restriction on the importation of iron is profitable to all home iron masters and iron workers; to lay restriction on the importation of linen goods is profitable to all in the linen trade; and so to lay restriction on woollen goods, to all who are in the woollen trade, etc.; and so to lay restrictions on all these and other articles will be favorable to the nation composed of such traders.

45. I believe this on the authority of my church, which is founded on the Word of God, which all the Church believes in.

46. It is clear that the United States do not acknowledge God as King of Nations, for they have nò Established Church.

Some one proposes what seems a good measure for the country at large; and it is shown that it will cause some people to grumble and a number of persons in the public service to be discharged.

Our forefathers, the wise and good in former generations, all believed this and acted on it, and I am satisfied to follow their example.

47. The theories of geologists cannot be true, for they tend to undermine our belief in Scripture.

48. I charge you with having started this calumny against me; and if you deny it, you must disprove the allegation.

49. I know that this man, that man, and others, all gained large sums at play; and surely I may do the same.

I have found on three occasions, when I had a dream of this kind, I heard soon after of the death of a friend. So when I dream in this way, I expect to hear of a death.

50. The institution has flourished under these rules; and it would be wrong in any one to attempt to change them.

51. Aut Sirius ardor;
Ille sitim morbosque ferens mortalibus ægris
Nascitur, et laevo contristat lumine cœlum.

The weather cannot be warmer till the snow is off the ground.

As long as the interest of money is so low, trade cannot be prosperous.

52. This story is likely to be true, for I had it from a man of fair character, who lived soon after the event (estimated value of testimony $\frac{9}{10}$), who probably had it from his father ($\frac{1}{3}$).

As each of the witnesses may possibly be wrong, we may believe them both to have been in error.

WORKS BY DR. McCOSH.

1 *THE METHOD OF THE DIVINE GOVERNMENT, PHYSICAL AND MORAL. 8vo. $2.50.*

"It is refreshing to read a work so distinguished for originality and soundness of thinking, especially as coming from an author of our own country."—*Sir Wm. Hamilton.*

"This work is distinguished from other similar ones by its being based upon a thorough study of physical science, and an accurate knowledge of its present condition, and by its entering in a deeper and more unfettered manner than its predecessors upon the discussion of the appropriate psychological, ethical, and theological questions. The author keeps aloof at once from the *à priori* idealism and dreaminess of German speculation since Schelling, and from the one-sidedness and narrowness of the empiricism and positivism which have so prevailed in England. In the provinces of psychology and ethics he follows conscientiously the facts of consciousness, and draws his conclusions of them commonly with penetration and logical certainty."—*Dr. Ulrici, in Zeitschrift für Philosophie.*

2. *TYPICAL FORMS AND SPECIAL ENDS IN CREATION. By JAMES McCOSH, LL.D., and DR. DICKIE. 8vo. $2.50.*

"It is alike comprehensive in its range, accurate and minute in its details, original in its structure, and devout and spirited in its tone and tendency. It illustrates and carries out the great principle of analogy in the Divine plans and works far more minutely and satisfactorily than it has been done before; and while it presents the results of the most profound scientific research, it presents them in their higher and spiritual relations."
—*Argus.*

3. *THE INTUITIONS OF THE MIND. New and Improved Edition. 8vo. $3.*

"No philosopher, before Dr. McCosh, has clearly brought out the stages by which an original and individual intuition passes first into an articulate but still individual judgment, and then into a universal maxim or principle; and no one has so clearly or completely classified and enumerated our intuitive convictions, or exhibited in detail their relations to the various sciences which repose on them as their foundations. The amount of summarized information which it contains is very great; and it is the only work on the very important subject with which it deals. Never was such a work so much needed as in the present day. It is the only scientific work adapted to counteract the school of Mill, Bain, and Herbert Spencer, which is so steadily prevailing among the students of the present generation."—*London Quarterly Review, April*, 1865.

4. *A DEFENCE OF FUNDAMENTAL TRUTH. Being an Examination of Mr. J. S. MILL'S Philosophy. 8vo. $3.*

"The spirit of these discussions is admirable. Fearless and courteous, McCosh never hesitates to bestow praise when merited, nor to attack a heresy wherever found."—*Cong. Review.*

5. *CHRISTIANITY AND POSITIVISM. A Series of Lectures. 12mo. $1.75.*

"As a practised dialectician, Dr. McCosh is a formidable opponent; and he brings to the defence of the truth a varied and extensive erudition. These Lectures are timely and valuable." — *Congregational Monthly.*

6. *ACADEMIC TEACHING IN EUROPE: Being DR. McCOSH'S Address at his Inauguration as President of the College of New Jersey. 50 cts.*

7 *LAWS OF DISCURSIVE THOUGHT: BEING A TEXT-BOOK OF FORMAL LOGIC. 12mo. $1.50.*

ROBERT CARTER & BROTHERS, New York

Any book on this Catalogue sent by mail, postage prepaid, on receipt of the price.

THEOLOGICAL, DEVOTIONAL,

AND

MISCELLANEOUS BOOKS,

PUBLISHED BY

ROBERT CARTER & BROTHERS,

530 Broadway, New York.

TO THE TRADE.—The discount on books marked thus (*) is smaller than on the others.

Able to Save;
Or, Encouragements to Patient Waiting. By the author of the "Pathway of Promise." Gilt $1.00

Abercrombie, John.
CONTEST AND THE ARMOR 50

Anderson, Christopher.
ANNALS OF THE ENGLISH BIBLE. 8vo 2.50
THE FAMILY BOOK 1.25

Arnot, William, D.D.
ON THE PARABLES 2.50
LIFE OF JAMES HAMILTON, D.D. 2.50

Assembly's Shorter Catechism. Per hundred 2.00
With proofs, per hundred 5.00

Baillie, Rev. John.
LIFE OF CAPTAIN BATE 75
LIFE STUDIES 60

Bickersteth, Rev. E. H.
YESTERDAY, TO-DAY, AND FOREVER. A Poem in 12 Books. 12mo . 2.00

"It is a sublime gospel poem, scholarly enough to meet the most fastidious taste, and plain enough to be understood by all; and interesting enough to hold the reader, of whatever class, to the end, and lead him to congratulate himself that he had met with such a work produced in the present century."—*Journal of Education.*

"It is truly wonderful in conception, sweet and beautiful in execution, and stirs the soul by the grand and awful revelations it brings before it. We do not hesitate to pronounce it the greatest sacred poem that has been written in modern times."—*S. S. Times.*

THE TWO BROTHERS, AND OTHER POEMS 2.00

"In this collection the author offers us some of his minor poems. . . . While differing considerably in merit, they all indicate the true poet. In some of the pieces there is the power of conception, and the distinctness of delineation, combined with skill in coloring, which clearly reveal the hand of a master."

Bickersteth, Rev. E. H.

The Blessed Dead, and the Risen Saints. 24mo, gilt $1.00
The Spirit of Life. 12mo 1.25
Waters from the Well-spring. 16mo 1.00

Bickersteth, Edward.

On the Lord's Supper 50

Blakely, Rev. John.

Theology of Inventions 1.25

Blunt, Rev. J. J.

Coincidences, and Paley's Horæ Paulinæ. In 1 vol. 1.50

"This work should be in the library of every Bible student. It comprises one of the very strongest arguments for the veracity of the Holy Scriptures." — *S. S. Journal*

Bogatzky's

Golden Treasury. 32mo, red edges. A beautiful edition 75

Bonar, Rev. Andrew A.

Commentary on Leviticus. 12mo 1.75
" " Psalms. 8vo 2.50
Visitor's Book of Texts 1.50

Bonar, Rev. Horatius, D.D.

Bible Thoughts and Themes. In 5 vols. 10.00

Or, separately:—

1. Old Testament . . . $2.00 | 3. Acts $2.00
2. Gospels . . . . . 2.00 | 4. Lesser Epistles . . . 2.00
5. Revelation $2.00

"This is a collection of condensed riches of Bible truth. The author has walked in the fields of the Old and New Testaments, and gathered a harvest of ripe fruits, which he spreads invitingly for the Christian reader. The volumes are beautifully printed on toned paper."

Hymns of Faith and Hope. 3 vols. 18mo, gilt top 2.25
" " " " Royal edition. 8vo 3.00

"Since Watts and Newton laid down their tuneful harps there has been no sweeter singer in Israel than Horatius Bonar. . . . Few writers of sacred song, of any age, have equalled him in simple beauty of thought and language, or in the terse presentation of great truths in poetic measure." — *Albany Evening Journal.*

God's Way of Peace 50
God's Way of Holiness 60
Night of Weeping 50
Morning of Joy 60
Story of Grace 50
Eternal Day .75
Family Sermons 1.75
Life of Rev. John Milne 2.00

Bonnet, L.

Family of Bethany 60

Booth, Rev. Abraham.

Reign of Grace 1.25

Book and its Story.

By L. N. R. 1.50

Borrow, George.

Bible and Gypsies of Spain 1.75

Boston, Rev. Thomas.

Select Works $3.00
Crook in the Lot 50
Fourfold State 75

Breckinridge, Rev. Robert J., D.D.

Knowledge of God Objectively considered 3.00
" " Subjectively " 3.50

"The plain practical Christian will be delighted with its tone of manly piety and its rich practical instruction. The man of literary taste and intellectual culture will enjoy the originality and boldness of the thought, and the profound and truly scientific spirit which characterizes it. The student of theology will rejoice in it as a real addition to theological science in this age of shams." — *Louisville Journal.*

Bridgeman, Mrs.

Daughters of China 75

Bridges, Rev. Charles.

On the Christian Ministry 2.50
An Exposition of the Proverbs 2.50

"The most lucid and satisfactory commentary on the Book of Proverbs that we have ever met."

Exposition of CXIX. Psalm 1.75

"Imbued with the essence of scriptural truth all over, insomuch that, as one passes from sentence to sentence, he might feel, as it were, the droppings of a heavenly manna upon the heart." — *Dr. Chalmers.*

Memoir of Mary Jane Graham 1.75

Broken Bud (The);

Or, The Reminiscences of a Bereaved Mother 1.25

Brooke, Rev. John T.

On Dancing 50

Brown, Rev. David,

On the Second Advent 1.75

Brown, John.

Concordance 50
Catechism, per hundred 2.00
Explication of the Assembly's Catechism. 12mo 1.00
" " " " 18mo 20

Brown, John, D.D.,

On First Peter. 8vo 3.50

"It has resolute adherence to the very truth of the passage, unforced development of the connection, and basing of edification on the right meaning of the Scripture. We have not met with any thing that surpasses it." — *North British Review.*

On the Discourses and Sayings of Christ. 2 vols. 8vo . . . 6.00

"We know not the book we could place beside these volumes, whether as a study and a model for the young minister, a library companion for the pastor, or a household instructor for the people of God." — *Evangelical Christendom.*

*On Romans. 8vo 2.50

"The author was distinguished for a rare union of qualities highly important to an interpreter of the Scriptures. He was a man of profound judgment and of deep piety. He had read extensively, and was particularly conversant with the best of books." — *Bibliotheca Sacra.*

Brown, John, M.D.,

ON HEALTH $0.50

Buchanan, Rev. James.

COMFORT IN AFFLICTION 60

Burns, Rev. W. C.

LIFE OF 2.50

"The most apostolic ministry, in our judgment, which the Church has seen since the apostolic days, was the ministry of William Burns. He literally went everywhere, "holding forth the word of life." He crossed oceans, learned strange languages, lived a solitary life, endured hardness as a good soldier of Jesus Christ, and made full proof of his ministry. He was as little entangled with the affairs of this life as any man who ever lived. Such characters and lives are rare, but they are needful for the instruction of the Church. We hope that the biography of this apostolic man will be studied thoroughly by the Church. It is beautifully portrayed in this volume." — *Presbyterian.*

Butler, Rev. C. M.,

ON THE APOCALYPSE 1.50

Butler, Bishop.

WORKS. Complete 2.50
ANALOGY. Separate 1.50
SERMONS " 1.75

"The 'Analogy' of Bishop Butler enjoys a reputation scarcely second to any other book than the Bible. As a specimen of analogical reasoning, we suppose it has never been equalled." — *N. E. Puritan.*

*Cabell, Dr. J. L.

UNITY OF MANKIND. 12mo 1.50

Caird's, Rev. John,

SERMONS 1.50

"The language of Mr. Caird's discourses is flowing, rich, and sparkling, often rising to the higher style of eloquence." — *Rev. Dr. Fish.*

Campbell, Rev. A. J.

POWER OF CHRIST TO SAVE 75

Cecil's Works.

Chalmers, Thomas, D.D.

SERMONS. 2 vols. 8vo 5.00

"So long as the eloquence of piety and truth illustrated by the loftiest powers of intellect and the largest acquisitions of learning shall have admiring students, so long will the writings of Chalmers stand in the front rank of religious literature, and be valued among the treasures of the Church of God." — *N. Y. Observer.*

LECTURES ON ROMANS. 8vo 2.50

"As a profound thinker and a powerful writer, — as an expositor of fundamental truth in divinity, — we are much deceived if he has his superior, or in all these respects his equal, among the divines of the present age and of any country." — *Boston Recorder.*

MISCELLANIES 2.50
ASTRONOMICAL AND COMMERCIAL DISCOURSES. In one vol. . . . 1.50

"His sketch of the glory of modern astronomy and its brilliant achievements is admirable, uniting the rapidity of a general survey with the precision of scientific truth." — *Albany Evening Journal.*

Chalmers, Thomas, D.D.

CHRISTIAN REVELATION. 2 vols. $2.50
NATURAL THEOLOGY. 2 vols. 2.50

Charlesworth, Miss.

THE LAST COMMAND 30

Charnock, Stephen,

ON THE ATTRIBUTES OF GOD. 8vo 3.50

"Perspicuity and depth, metaphysical subtlety and evangelical simplicity, immense learning and plain but irrefragable reasoning, conspire to render this work one of the most inestimable productions that ever did honor to the sanctified judgment and genius of a human being." — *Toplady.*

Cheever, Rev. Geo. B.

LECTURES ON BUNYAN. 12mo 2.00

"Dr. Cheever's name will go down to posterity conjoined with the immortal dreamer, in a union no less intimate, though more honorable, than that of Johnson and Boswell. As a commentator of Bunyan, he stands without peer or rival." — *Christian Chronicle.*

LECTURES ON COWPER 1.50
BIBLE IN THE COMMON SCHOOLS 1.25

Clark, John A., D.D.

WALK ABOUT ZION 1.25
GATHERED FRAGMENTS 1.50
YOUNG DISCIPLE 1.50
PASTOR'S TESTIMONY 1.25
AWAKE, THOU SLEEPER 1.25

Clarke, Samuel, D.D.

SCRIPTURE PROMISES 50

Collier, Rev. Joseph.

DAWN OF HEAVEN 1.50

Cripple of Antioch.

By the author of the "Schönberg-Cotta Family" 1.00

Cuyler, Rev. T. L.

THOUGHT-HIVES. 12mo 1.75

"Good nature, human sympathy, and Christian zeal kindle all his pages into a magnetic warmth. Genial, open-hearted, and fascinating in his style, both spoken and written, he has made for himself a land-wide reputation, and written his name everywhere as a household word." — *Evangelist.*

THE CEDAR CHRISTIAN. 16mo 90

"Many of these papers are intense, they are all clear and forcible, and some of them are replete with that grace which comes of fervor, — that soft and mellow light which the fancy throws around what the heart sees as well as the eyes." — *Brooklyn Union.*

THE EMPTY CRIB. A Book of Consolation. 24mo 1.00

"The most beautiful little gift for bereaved parents is the Rev. Mr. Cuyler's tribute to his Georgie, — the 'Empty Crib.' A saintly bunch of white lilies is it from full hands and hearts." — *Zion's Herald.*

STRAY ARROWS. 18mo 60

D'Aubigné, J. H. Merle, D.D.

THE HISTORY OF THE REFORMATION. 5 vols. 12mo $6.00
" " " " all in 1 vol. 3.00

"Without doing any violence to historical truth, he invests history with all the charms of a dignified romance. He writes as one whose own soul has been stirred by what he describes. His characters and scenes have deeply impressed his mind; and, with the enthusiasm and skill of the poet, he sketches on the historic page his fascinating, life-like pictures."

THE HISTORY OF THE REFORMATION IN THE TIME OF CALVIN. 5 vols. 10.00

"Part of a work that will live through all time. Apart from the charms of a pleasing and fluent style, pictorial diction, and intense vitality, its accurate erudition, careful statements, judicial impartiality, and eager appreciation of good in any connection, are merits entitling to immortality. It is a brilliant and powerful history of one of the greatest revolutions in human affairs and prospects." — *Christian Advocate.*

Daily Commentary

FOR FAMILY WORSHIP. By 180 Clergymen of Scotland 2.50

David's Psalms in Metre.

12mo, cloth	$1.25	18mo, cloth, gilt . . .	$0.75
" " gilt . . .	1.50	48mo, cloth	.30
" *Turkey morocco .	4.50	" " gilt . . .	.40
18mo, cloth	.60	" Sheep	.40
With Brown's Notes . .	.75		

Davies', Samuel,

SERMONS. 3 vols. 3.75

"I most sincerely wish that young ministers more especially would peruse these volumes with the deepest attention and seriousness, and endeavor to form their discourses according to the model of our author." — *Rev. Thomas Gibbons.*

Dick, Thomas, D.D.

LECTURES ON THEOLOGY. Complete in 1 volume. 8vo 3.50

"We recommend this work in the very strongest terms to the Biblical student. It is, as a whole, superior to any other system of theology in our language. As an elementary book, especially fitted for those who are commencing the study of divinity, it is unrivalled." — *Christian Journal.*

LECTURES ON THE ACTS 2.25

*Doddridge, Rev. Philip.

FAMILY EXPOSITOR ON THE NEW TESTAMENT. Royal 8vo. Sheep .

Drummond, Rev. D. T. K.

ON THE PARABLES. New edition. Large 12mo 1.75

*Dublin Tracts.

Per packet 1.00

Duchess of Gordon,

MEMOIR OF 1.25

Duncan, Rev. Henry.

PHILOSOPHY OF THE SEASONS. 2 vols. 3.00

www.ingramcontent.com/pod-product-compliance
Lightning Source LLC
LaVergne TN
LVHW012327100826
845148LV00017B/392

* 9 7 8 1 4 2 5 5 2 0 9 4 6 *